THE KEY
STUDENT STUDY GUIDE

THE KEY student study guide is designed to help students achieve success in school. The content in each study guide is 100% curriculum aligned and serves as an excellent source of material for review and practice. To create this book, teachers, curriculum specialists, and assessment experts have worked closely to develop the instructional pieces that explain each of the key concepts for the course. The practice questions and sample tests have detailed solutions that show problem-solving methods, highlight concepts that are likely to be tested, and point out potential sources of errors. **THE KEY** is a complete guide to be used by students throughout the school year for reviewing and understanding course content, and to prepare for assessments.

S0-AUT-323

Copyright Protected

Copyright © 2000–2016 by Castle Rock Research Corporation. All rights reserved. No part of this book covered by the copyright hereon may be reproduced or used in any form or by any means graphic, electronic, or mechanical, including photocopying, recording, taping, or information storage and retrieval systems without the express permission of the publisher.

Publisher
Gautam Rao

Contributors
Anthony Regan
Richard Walker

Reviewers
Samantha Frampton
Lois Westerlund

Rao, Gautam, 1961 –
THE KEY– English 10-1
ISBN: 978-1-77044-424-9

    1. English – Juvenile Literature. I. Title

Published by
Castle Rock Research Corp.
2000 First & Jasper
10065 Jasper Avenue
Edmonton, AB T5J 3B1

10 9 8 7 6 5

CASTLE ROCK
RESEARCH CORP

Dedicated to the memory of Dr. V. S. Rao

Not for Reproduction

THE KEY—English 10-1

THE KEY consists of the following sections:

KEY Tips for Being Successful at School gives examples of study and review strategies. It includes information about learning styles, study schedules, and note taking for test preparation.

Class Focus includes a unit on each area of the curriculum. Units are divided into sections, each focusing on one of the specific expectations, or main ideas, that students must learn about in that unit. **Examples, definitions, and visuals help to explain each main idea.** The Practice Tests are prefaced by a Tables of Correlations. Answers and solutions are found at the end of each unit.

KEY Strategies for Success on Tests helps students get ready for tests. It shows students different types of questions they might see, word clues to look for when reading them, and hints for answering them.

Practice Tests includes one to three tests based on the entire course. They are very similar to the format and level of difficulty that students may encounter on final tests. In some regions, these tests may be reprinted versions of official tests, or reflect the same difficulty levels and formats as official versions. This gives students the chance to practice using real-world examples. Answers and complete solutions are provided at the end of the section.

For the complete curriculum document (including specific expectations along with examples and sample problems), visit http://education.alberta.ca/teachers/program/english/programs.aspx

THE KEY *Study Guides* are available for many courses. Check www.castlerockresearch.com for a complete listing of books available for your area.

For information about any of our resources or services, please call Castle Rock Research at 780.448.9619 or visit our website at http://www.castlerockresearch.com.

At Castle Rock Research, we strive to produce an error-free resource. If you should find an error, please contact us so that future editions can be corrected.

Copyright Protected

TABLE OF CONTENTS

KEY Tips for Being Successful at School

Not for Reproduction

KEY TIPS FOR BEING SUCCESSFUL AT SCHOOL

KEY FACTORS CONTRIBUTING TO SCHOOL SUCCESS

In addition to learning the content of your courses, there are some other things that you can do to help you do your best at school. You can try some of the following strategies:

- **Keep a positive attitude**: Always reflect on what you can already do and what you already know.

- **Be prepared to learn**: Have the necessary pencils, pens, notebooks, and other required materials for participating in class ready.

- **Complete all of your assignments**: Do your best to finish all of your assignments. Even if you know the material well, practice will reinforce your knowledge. If an assignment or question is difficult for you, work through it as far as you can so that your teacher can see exactly where you are having difficulty.

- **Set small goals for yourself when you are learning new material**: For example, when learning the parts of speech, do not try to learn everything in one night. Work on only one part or section each study session. When you have memorized one particular part of speech and understand it, move on to another one. Continue this process until you have memorized and learned all the parts of speech.

- **Review your classroom work regularly at home**: Review to make sure you understand the material you learned in class.

- **Ask your teacher for help**: Your teacher will help you if you do not understand something or if you are having a difficult time completing your assignments.

- **Get plenty of rest and exercise**: Concentrating in class is hard work. It is important to be well-rested and have time to relax and socialize with your friends. This helps you keep a positive attitude about your schoolwork.

- **Eat healthy meals**: A balanced diet keeps you healthy and gives you the energy you need for studying at school and at home.

HOW TO FIND YOUR LEARNING STYLE

Every student learns differently. The manner in which you learn best is called your learning style. By knowing your learning style, you can increase your success at school. Most students use a combination of learning styles. Do you know what type of learner you are? Read the following descriptions. Which of these common learning styles do you use most often?

- Do you need to say things out loud? You may learn best by saying, hearing, and seeing words. You are probably really good at memorizing things such as dates, places, names, and facts. You may need to write down the steps in a process, a formula, or the actions that lead up to a significant event, and then say them out loud.

- Do you need to read or see things? You may learn best by looking at and working with pictures. You are probably really good at puzzles, imagining things, and reading maps and charts. You may need to use strategies like mind mapping and webbing to organize your information and study notes.

- Do you need to draw or write things down? You may learn best by touching, moving, and figuring things out using manipulatives. You are probably really good at physical activities and learning through movement. You may need to draw your finger over a diagram to remember it, tap out the steps needed to solve a problem, or feel yourself writing or typing a formula.

Copyright Protected

Not for Reproduction

SCHEDULING STUDY TIME

You should review your class notes regularly to ensure that you have a clear understanding of all the new material you learned. Reviewing your lessons on a regular basis helps you to learn and remember ideas and concepts. It also reduces the quantity of material that you need to study prior to a test. Establishing a study schedule will help you to make the best use of your time.

- Regardless of the type of study schedule you use, you may want to consider the following suggestions to maximize your study time and effort:

- Organize your work so that you begin with the most challenging material first.

- Divide the subject's content into small, manageable chunks.

- Alternate regularly between your different subjects and types of study activities in order to maintain your interest and motivation.

- Make a daily list with headings like "Must Do," "Should Do," and "Could Do."

- Begin each study session by quickly reviewing what you studied the day before.

- Maintain your usual routine of eating, sleeping, and exercising to help you concentrate better for extended periods of time.

Copyright Protected

CREATING STUDY NOTES

MIND-MAPPING OR WEBBING

Use the key words, ideas, or concepts from your class notes to create a mind map or web, which is a diagram or visual representation of the given information. A mind map or web is sometimes referred to as a knowledge map. Use the following steps to create a mind map or web:

1. Write the key word, concept, theory, or formula in the centre of your page.

2. Write down related facts, ideas, events, and information, and link them to the central concept with lines.

3. Use coloured markers, underlining, or symbols to emphasize things such as relationships, timelines, and important information.

The following mind map is an example of one that could help you develop an essay:

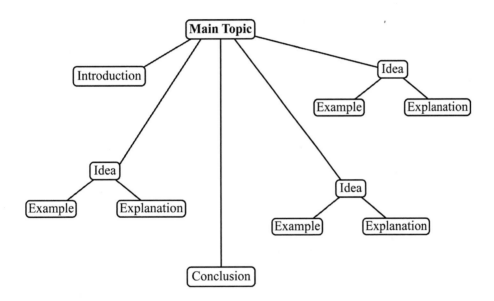

Not for Reproduction

INDEX CARDS

To use index cards while studying, follow these steps:

1. Write a key word or question on one side of an index card.

2. On the reverse side, write the definition of the word, answer to the question, or any other important information that you want to remember.

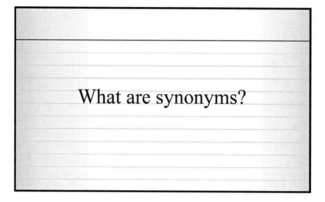

SYMBOLS AND STICKY NOTES—IDENTIFYING IMPORTANT INFORMATION

Use symbols to mark your class notes. For example, an exclamation mark (!) might be used to point out something that must be learned well because it is a very important idea. A question mark (?) may highlight something you are not certain about, and a diamond (◊) or asterisk (*) could highlight interesting information that you want to remember. Sticky notes are useful in the following situations:

• Use sticky notes when you are not allowed to put marks in books.

• Use sticky notes to mark a page in a book that contains an important diagram, formula, explanation, or other information.

• Use sticky notes to mark important facts in research books.

Copyright Protected

MEMORIZATION TECHNIQUES

The following techniques can help you when you need to memorize something:

- **Association** relates new learning to something you already know. For example, to remember the spelling difference between dessert and desert, recall that the word *sand* has only one *s*. So, because there is sand in a desert, the word *desert* has only one *s*.

- **Mnemonic** devices are sentences that you create to remember a list or group of items. For example, the first letter of each word in the phrase "**E**very **G**ood **B**oy **D**eserves **F**udge" helps you to remember the names of the lines on the treble-clef staff (E, G, B, D, and F) in music.

- **Acronyms** are words that are formed from the first letters or parts of the words in a group. For example, RADAR is actually an acronym for Radio Detecting and Ranging, and MASH is an acronym for Mobile Army Surgical Hospital. HOMES helps you to remember the names of the five Great Lakes (Huron, Ontario, Michigan, Erie, and Superior).

- **Visualizing** requires you to use your mind's eye to "see" a chart, list, map, diagram, or sentence as it is in your textbook or notes, on the chalkboard or computer screen, or in a display.

- **Initialisms** are abbreviations that are formed from the first letters or parts of the words in a group. Unlike acronyms, an initialism cannot be pronounced as a word itself. For example, BEDMAS is an initialism for the order of operations in math (Brackets, Exponents, Divide, Multiply, Add, Subtract).

KEY STRATEGIES FOR REVIEWING

Reviewing textbook material, class notes, and handouts should be an ongoing activity. Spending time reviewing becomes more critical when you are preparing for a test. You may find some of the following review strategies useful when studying during your scheduled study time:

- Before reading a selection, preview it by noting the headings, charts, graphs, and chapter questions.

- Before reviewing a unit, note the headings, charts, graphs, and chapter questions.

- Highlight key concepts, vocabulary, definitions, and formulas.

- Skim the paragraph, and note the key words, phrases, and information.

- Carefully read over each step in a procedure.

- Draw a picture or diagram to help make the concept clearer.

Not for Reproduction

KEY STRATEGIES FOR SUCCESS: A CHECKLIST

Reviewing is a huge part of doing well at school and preparing for tests. Here is a checklist for you to keep track of how many suggested strategies for success you are using. Read each question, and put a check mark (✓) in the correct column. Look at the questions where you have checked the "No" column. Think about how you might try using some of these strategies to help you do your best at school.

KEY Strategies for Success	Yes	No
Do you attend school regularly?		
Do you know your personal learning style—how you learn best?		
Do you spend 15 to 30 minutes a day reviewing your notes?		
Do you study in a quiet place at home?		
Do you clearly mark the most important ideas in your study notes?		
Do you use sticky notes to mark texts and research books?		
Do you practise answering multiple-choice and written-response questions?		
Do you ask your teacher for help when you need it?		
Are you maintaining a healthy diet and sleep routine?		
Are you participating in regular physical activity?		

Reading and Writing

READING AND WRITING

DEFINITIONS

Representation is defined by Alberta Education to include such things as a picture, collage, video, chart, diagram, or poster and certain kinds of performance such as tableaux and mime. Representation is also defined as including music and tone of voice when these are used to produce mood or atmosphere. This production is called *text creation*.

Texts are the things that students listen to, read, and view. *Text* is defined by Alberta Education as any kind of communication in oral, print, visual, or multimedia form. Thus conversation is *oral text*, words written on paper are *print text*, photographs are *visual text*, and drum dancing and cartoon strips are examples of *multimedia text*. Authors, playwrights, photographers, cartoonists, and choreographers are all *text creators*.

This definition is not the common definition. Most people understand *text* to mean words written on a page. For example, your science book contains both text and illustrations, and most people think of these as two different things but using the Alberta Education definition, they are both text. This is a specialized meaning of the term of which students should be aware.

Context is perhaps a more familiar term. It has two closely related meanings. In a sentence, all the words before and after a particular word are the word's context. The context helps to explain the word's meaning. The same is true of all the words before or after a phrase, a paragraph, or an entire chapter.

Here is a stage direction from *Romeo and Juliet*.

- *Enter an officer, and three or four Citizens with clubs or partisans.*

What is a *partisan*? The other word in the same context is *clubs*. The context makes it clear that clubs will do as well as partisans. Students can safely guess that a partisan is a weapon.

Context can also mean the entire situation in which something exists. This kind of context also helps to explain meaning. Everything that happens has a context.

- *The destruction of the World Trade Centre towers on September 11, 2001 must be understood in the context of world history.*

Copyright Protected

Texts also have context. A text is produced in a certain time and place and for a certain reason. Knowing the context may help the reader, the viewer, or the listener to better understand the situation as in the following examples and explanation:

- *In 1816, Mary Shelley had a nightmare vision of a young student constructing a monster. The nightmare led to her writing* Frankenstein. *The fact that she had the nightmare had a context: she and her companions had been telling ghost and horror stories for days. The content of her nightmare also had a context: Mary Shelley lived in a time of rapid change, when scientific advances were making many people uneasy. Widespread doubts about the reckless pursuit of knowledge help to explain the things she saw in her vision.*

You will use both kinds of context frequently in English Language Arts 10-1.

FORM AND GENRE

Genre sometimes means any classification of texts by **form**, **style**, or **subject matter**. However, a more careful definition distinguishes between **form** and **genre**.

Form describes structure.

Examples of Forms	Characteristics
Letter	Generally begins with an inside address and date; uses conventional greeting and closings like *Dear* _____ and *Yours sincerely*
Memorandum	Often brief and addressed to a limited group such as the employees of a company; limited to essential information
Short story	20 000 words or less; usually few characters, one main character; a single plot
Novella	20 000 to 50 000 words; a shorter version of a novel
Novel	Over 50 000 words; usually 90 000 to 100 000 or more; may contain many characters and multiple plots within the main story
Screenplay	Contains mainly dialogue and directions for the action; special rules for margins and font size give a standard length of approximately one page to one minute of screen-time

Genre describes *content*, or *subject matter*.

Genres contain certain characteristic elements. A western usually includes a gunfight. Science fiction often includes imaginary scientific developments like interstellar spaceships. A romance is always complicated with misunderstandings and difficulties.

Forms and genres are combined in various ways. For example, an **epistolary novel**, a novel told through letters, is a combination of two forms. Such a novel could be written in any genre and genres can be combined. A science fiction story might also be a romance, and an historical novel might also be a detective story. Also, elements of one genre are sometimes used in different genres.

Copyright Protected

There are many possible combinations of form and genre. The following chart shows a few of the more common examples.

Examples of Forms			Examples of Genres
Fiction	Poetry	Metrical Free verse sonnet	Epic Ballad Lyric
	Prose	Play Musical Motion picture Shakespearean Modern	Tragedy Comedy
		Novel Novella Short story	Historical Detective Fantasy Science fiction Realistic
Non-fiction		History	Political Social Military
		Biography Autobiography Memoir	
		Documentary film	
		Essay	Expository Persuasive Research
		Letter	Personal Business Letter to the editor
		Diary	
		References	Encyclopedia Dictionary Thesaurus Atlas
		Textbook Manual	

The choice of form depends on the author's purpose and on the expected audience.

Not for Reproduction

READING NARRATIVES

All stories, or **narratives**, have certain things in common. Short stories, novels, and movies, even history books and documentaries, share certain common elements. Some elements may be more developed in one kind of narrative. Non-fiction, for example, imposes certain limits such as telling the truth. However, you can expect the following elements in most works that you read or view.

POINT OF VIEW

A story always has a narrator: someone who tells the story. **Narrative point of view** describes who tells the story and how the story is told. In one sense, the real narrator is the author. However, the narrator is also one of the author's invented characters, made up just as the author made up the story. The chart summarizes key concepts regarding the narrative points of view.

Point of View	How the Story is Told	Narrators
First person	• The story is told by one of the characters in the story ("I"). • The narrator is part of the story.	• **First-person narrators** only know what they themselves think, feel, do, and see.
Third person	• The story is told through the eyes of one or more characters ("he, she, they"). • The narrator is outside the story, and tells what the characters think, feel, and do.	• **Omniscient narrators** know about everything that happens and what every character knows, thinks, feels, and does. • **Limited-omniscient narrators** only know about one character and the things that one character knows, thinks, feels, and does.
Objective	• The story is told without telling any characters' thoughts and feelings. Only the characters' actions and words are told. • This point of view is like the camera's point of view in a film.	• The **objective narrator** only knows what a camera can record. This story-telling form suffers from the limitations of film, but, at the same time, can produce a film-like effect.

Sometimes the narrator cannot be trusted. In telling the story, the narrator may make mistakes, misunderstand things, leave things out, or tell lies. The **unreliable narrator** is a good example of the author inventing the narrator.

The narrator may sometimes address the reader directly, as in Charlotte Brontë's *Jane Eyre*, when the first-person narrator says *Reader, I married him.* While stories are commonly told without direct comment, first-person narrators often comment indirectly by simply telling their thoughts.

Copyright Protected

PLOT

A **plot** is made up of two things: the events of the story and the reasons for the events. In telling about a book or a movie many people say *X happened and then Y happened and then Z happened.* However, without knowing *why* X, Y, and Z happened, there is no plot; there is only a list of events.

The causes of events are an important part of a plot.

Most plots also have a recognizable structure. The following elements can be recognized in nearly every plot.

1. Exposition

- Introduction of characters, setting, and situation
- Explanation of **antecedent action**, or what happened before the story started

2. Complication

- Increasing **conflict**
- **Characterization**, or development of characters

3. Climax

- The turning point
- The culmination of the conflict, action, or series of events

4. Resolution

- Final explanations and conclusion
- Sometimes called the **denouement**, or final outcome which explains everything
- Sometimes divided into denouement and resolution

These plot elements are often outlined in a **plot diagram**.

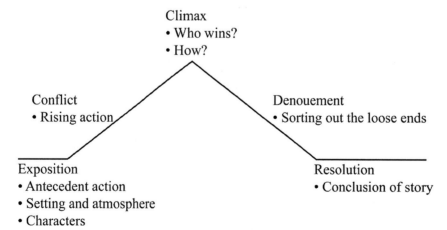

Either the plot elements or the plot diagram can be used to outline nearly everything that occurs in a short story. When studying a novel, the plot is longer and more complicated, and there may be subplots. In addition, chapters of a book can also be outlined using plot structure. As a result, a novel study might require several plot outlines: one for the plot of the overall story, one or more for subplots, and a number for plotting each chapter or other divisions of the story.

CONFLICT

Stories are about people and their struggles. In a story, everything that gets in the way of characters as they struggle to get what they want, produces **conflict**. Sometimes the conflict can be physical struggles or dramatic disagreements. Conflict may also exist in misunderstanding and uncertainty. In a mystery story, the mystery itself can be the conflict. Conflicts may be internal or external, as summarized in the following chart.

Internal	External
• Characters struggle within *themselves*. They struggle with conscience, emotions, destructive character traits, or with conflicting desires or principles. • Internal conflict can be complicated and may also be combined with external conflict. An inner conflict over values, for example, can be part of a conflict with society's values.	• Characters may struggle with *other people* because of hatred, disagreement, or misunderstanding. There may be a struggle between good and evil. There may be conflicting ideas about what is good, such as a clash of ideals. It is even possible for all the characters to be working together while problems arise from "the conflict." • Characters may struggle with entire groups of people, or the conflict may be with *society*. • Characters may struggle with *universal problems* like war, disease, poverty, or alienation. • Characters may struggle with *nature* in the form of unusual weather, hostile terrain, or savage animals. • Characters may struggle with the *unknown*, with mysteries of any kind: ghosts, miracles, alien abductions, fate, the final mystery of death or with the theft of a diamond necklace.

CHARACTERIZATION

Everything that a writer does to portray characters is called *characterization*. One of the basic methods of characterization is to invent different kinds of characters that serve different purposes. Characters can be classified by type and function.

Characters Classified by Type

Flat	Have only one quality or character trait; are one-sided; always act the same way
Round	Have different, even contradictory traits; are more like real people
Stock	Are like flat characters, except that stock characters have been used over and over and are instantly recognizable
Archetypal	Are like stock characters, except that *archetypes* are meant to be typical (even universal) examples of certain character traits
Dynamic	Change or grow in some way either for good or bad; are altered by events and by their own actions and choices
Static	Do not change; *flat, round, stock,* and *archetypal* characters can all be static
Foil	Used as a contrast to the main character or protagonist; the difference between the foil and the main character emphasizes the main character's qualities; the foil is used for **indirect characterization**

Good storytellers use all of these types of characters. The most important character in a story is usually rounded and dynamic. However, the taxi driver whose only function is to delay the protagonist by taking a wrong turn is usually flat. In fact, some characters must be flat, as there is no time or space to portray them as real people.

The amount of characterization that a character receives is generally controlled by the character's function in the story.

Characters Classified by Function

Protagonist	The main character; often the hero, but not always, as sometimes the main character is a villain; often a **dynamic character**
Antagonist	The character the protagonist struggles against; often the villain, but not always
Major	Help move the plot forward in some way; they are often round and dynamic; the **protagonist** and **antagonist** are major characters
Minor	Have minor roles; they affect an event in the plot, but they do not move the whole plot forward; are often **flat** or **stock** because they do not appear long enough to be fully developed

Writers have two ways of portraying their characters. They can comment directly, or they can show their characters speaking and acting.

Methods of Characterization

Direct characterization is told through direct statements made by the narrator.	Indirect characterization is shown through actions and dialogue.
• From the narrator's statements about a character, e.g. "Jane was clever and stubborn." • From indirect characterization that is obvious or contrived, as when one character says or thinks something about another character, and it sounds just like the narrator's voice, or when a character stops to look in a mirror	• From what a character says or thinks • From what a character says or thinks about another character • From what a character thinks about self, others, and the world • From what a character does • From a character's reactions to a character

SETTING AND ATMOSPHERE

The **setting** is the *where* and *when*: present-day New York, the American South in 1850, the moon in 2135, the African veldt in the Stone Age, Renaissance Verona. When a story is carefully constructed, the setting is an important part of the work.

The setting is often chosen for a purpose. Think of the setting of the scene in Shakespeare's *Macbeth* in which Macbeth and Banquo meet the three witches. The setting is a heath, a land so infertile that it will not even support trees. A wasteland emphasizes the evil of the witches who are cut off from human society by their crimes, just as Macbeth's crimes will soon cut him off from society.

The **atmosphere** is the mood or the feeling produced by a work. The feeling of gloom, horror, and despair that afflicts Macbeth as he sinks deeper into crime is the atmosphere of the play; it is the feeling that the play produces in the audience.

The setting often contributes to the atmosphere. Sometimes both setting and atmosphere can be deliberately arranged to contrast with the events or meaning of a story.

THEME

The **theme** of any work is its subject, what the work is about. The theme can be divided into two parts: the subject itself and what is said about the subject. For example, Shakespeare's *Macbeth* is about ambition, and that ambition is pursued ruthlessly, at the cost of many lives. Shakespeare shows that once Macbeth decides to be king, he commits one crime after another to first seize the throne and then to keep it.

The theme can be described in a kind of equation.

$$\boxed{\text{Subject}} \; + \; \boxed{\text{Statement about the subject}} \; = \; \boxed{\text{Theme}}$$

In a skilfully constructed narrative, everything contributes to the theme. Everything in the narrative is about the theme.

All the elements of the narrative contribute to the theme.

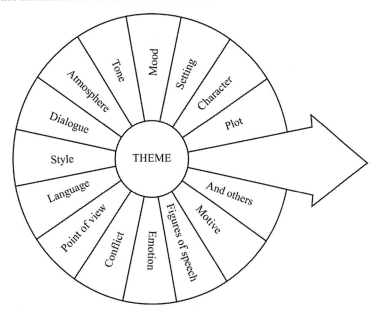

The **moral** of a story and its theme are connected, but they are not the same. A moral is a conclusion drawn from events in a story. It is a statement about the best way to behave. If a story has a moral, then sometimes the author states it. It is more common for the moral to be left for the reader to discover.

READING POETRY

A **poem** is a piece of writing that presents vivid experiences, ideas, or emotions by appealing to the imagination of the reader. Poems produce their effect through the use of images, sounds, and rhythm. They frequently contain poetic devices, such **alliteration** and **onomatopoeia** (two sound devices), and figures of speech, such as **metaphor** and **simile** (two ways of making comparisons). Poems often contain **allusions**, or indirect mention of things such as other literature or history.

Copyright Protected

All of these characteristics can make poetry less appealing to read, and for some, more difficult to understand. However, poetry can be enjoyable and rewarding. There is a reason many people, not just poets, write poems to express themselves in moments of grief or triumph. Think of the heartfelt poems written for a funeral or for graduation.

Since a poem is so densely packed with layers of meaning and poetic techniques, reading poetry is an exercise in unpacking the layers. Here is a way of reading a poem that many people find useful.

Read a poem more than once, each time paying attention to a different level of meaning.

First, understand the words themselves, then the imagery, then the symbols, then the allusions, and then the poetic techniques.

Finally, the meaning of the entire poem should be easier to understand and appreciate.

Here is an outline of the method.

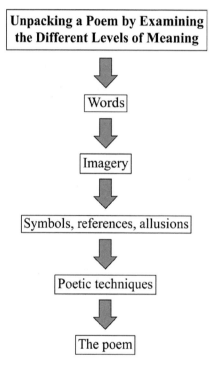

You might find that understanding the words and understanding the imagery go together. Or you might find that the order of understanding is different for different poems and for different readers. That is to be expected. This way of reading a poem is a suggestion. Use the method or adapt it.

UNDERSTANDING POETRY

Here is an example of how to read a poem written by Marjorie Pickthall (1883–1922), an English and Canadian poet and writer.

STARS

Now in the West the slender moon lies low,
And now Orion glimmers through the trees,
Clearing the earth with even pace and slow,
And now the stately-moving Pleiades,
5 In that soft infinite darkness overhead
Hang jewel-wise upon a silver thread.

And all the lonelier stars that have their place,
Calm lamps within the distant southern sky,
And planet-dust upon the edge of space,
10 Look down upon the fretful world, and I
Look up to outer vastness unafraid
And see the stars which sang when earth was made.

—*by* Marjorie Pickthall

Understand the Words

Understanding the meaning of each word is the first step in understanding the whole poem. Here are the words that might need to be looked up, or noticed and thought about.

the West	a compass direction; when capitalized, represents a region
slender moon	crescent moon: moon either waxing or waning
glimmer	give a faint, intermittent light
stately	impressive, dignified, graceful
pace	speed of walking, running, or other movement
Orion, the Pleiades	two constellations, or groups of stars often named after characters from Greek mythology; Orion was a hunter, and the Pleiades were seven sisters
-wise	in a certain way, direction, or manner
jewel-wise	in the way that a jewel does
planet-dust	vast dust clouds in space compressed by gravity to form planets and stars
edge of space	since the time of the ancient Greeks, the universe is known to be vast; edge of space might be figure of speech, or might be meant to be accurate according to the knowledge of the time
fretful	agitated, disturbed

Copyright Protected

Understand the Imagery

The author's emotional response to the night sky and to all of life is carefully created through a series of images. She looks up at the night sky and she sees the moon and stars.

slender moon lies low	crescent moon is setting
Orion glimmers through the trees	stars are seen through branches: the leaves must have fallen; it is fall or winter
clears the earth	constellation is rising in the east
overhead	the Pleiades rise before Orion and are high in the sky; the placement of the moon and stars are correct for a night in November in the early 1900s
jewel-wise upon a silver thread	stars like jewels are compared to a necklace; thread is an allusion to star charts that show the stars connected with lines; the entire image recalls the beauty of diamonds and silver

The night sky is **personified**, or given human characteristics. Words like *slender*, *even pace*, *stately-moving*, *lonelier*, *calm*, and *look down* all make the heavenly bodies appear to be alive and aware. The images are all beautiful and peaceful: *the Pleiades, / In that soft infinite darkness overhead / Hang jewel-wise upon a silver thread.*

Understand the Symbols, References, and Allusions

Poetry often includes elements that refer to things other than themselves.

A **symbol** is something that stands for something else, especially for something abstract. In this poem, the stars are symbols of peace, order, and purpose.

A **reference** is a direct mention of something that is related to whatever is being discussed. The mention of *Romeo and Juliet* at the beginning of this **KEY** is an example of a reference. However, the images and references in this poem are indirect.

An **allusion** is an indirect reference. Because it is indirect, an allusion can be more difficult to recognize and understand. Writers and poets often expect their readers to have certain knowledge or to be familiar with certain events or writings. References and allusions often refer to historical, mythological, and religious subjects.

Line 1 may contain an allusion to the World War One slang to *go west*, which means *to die*. The term itself is an allusion to the death toll on the Western Front. If the moon is *waning*, becoming less, then *slender moon* would support this interpretation. The moon is certainly setting, which does support the interpretation. All this accounts for the capitalization of *west*, a word that is not capitalized when used as a direction.

This poem was published **posthumously**, after the author's death in 1925. Depending on when she wrote or last worked on poem, *the West* (line 1) may be a symbol of death.

Lines 10 and 11 contain an allusion to Blaise Pascal's (a 17th century French mathematician, scientist, and religious philosopher) famous words about the vastness of space: *The eternal silence of these infinite spaces terrifies me.* Marjorie Pickthall, however, feels the opposite: *I look up to outer vastness unafraid.*

Line 12 is an allusion to the Book of Job from the Bible, when God speaks to Job about the creation of the earth, *When the morning stars sang together, and all the sons of God shouted for joy.* Job, like the *fretful world* (line 10) had suffered greatly, and this line about the creation of the world is part of the response to his suffering.

Understand the Poetic Techniques

A **lyric** is a short poem expressing personal thoughts and feelings. Clearly, "Stars" is a lyric poem.

"Stars" is divided into two sections, or **stanzas**, like paragraphs. Stanzas have the same function as paragraphs. Notice that the first stanza is a description of what the writer sees in the night sky, while the second is a description of her reaction to what she sees. The poem has a regular rhyme scheme. In each **stanza**, or group of verses, the last words of each **verse**, or line of poetry, rhyme in an *ababcc* pattern. The regularity of the rhyme scheme matches the regular movement of the stars in the night sky.

Lines 1–4 and 7–9 are all **end-stopped**; they end with a comma that indicates a pause. Lines 5, 10, and 11, however, have no end punctuation. The thought continues without a pause into the next line. This technique, called **enjambment**, varies the rhythm of the poem to avoid monotony and it emphasizes the enjambed lines. In this poem, the enjambment is used at the end of each stanza to emphasize the most important idea. It also varies the regular rhythm.

"Stars" is written with a regular rhythm. It is an example of **metrical**, or traditional poetry.

Metrical or Traditional Poetry

Not all poetry rhymes, but nearly all poetry has strong rhythm. Finding that rhythm allows you to read the poem as the author intended it to be read. The rhythm often provides clues to meaning. This is especially true if the poet has used irregular **syntax** (sentence structure) or complicated imagery.

The basis of rhythm in metrical poetry should be understood. First, recall how a dictionary shows words divided into syllables. The stressed syllables are marked with accents: re•mem′•ber, com′•men•tar′•y. In metrical poetry, the regular alternation of stressed and unstressed syllables produces the regular rhythm. The rhythm of poetry is called **meter** and a unit of rhythm is called a **foot**. Certain metrical feet have names. Here are the two most common.

- Iambic foot: *unstressed, **stressed** (today, abstain, the **right**)*

- Trochaic foot: ***stressed**, unstressed (**coun**ter, **chem**ist, **once** upon a **mid**night)*

A line of metrical poetry is usually made up of a fixed number of feet. Thus a poem written **in iambic pentameter**, the most common meter in English-language metrical poetry, has lines of five **iambs**. (*Penta* is Greek for five and an iamb has two syllables. Thus, the average line has ten syllables.)

Because poets pattern words into a regular rhythm, that rhythm can be indicated with stress marks above syllables:

- "—" above an unaccented syllable (weak stress)

- " / " above an accented syllable (strong stress).

This kind of careful examination of the rhythm of a poem is called **scansion**. Here is the first stanza, **scanned**.

```
     —    /    —     /    —    /    —     /     —    /
1    Now  in   the   West the  slen der  moon  lies low,

     —    /    —     /    —    /    —     /     —    /
2    And  now  O     ri   on   glim mers through the  trees,

     /    —    —     /    —    /    —     /     —    /
3    Clear ing  the  earth with e   ven  pace  and  slow,

     —    /    —     /    —    /    —     /     —    /
4    And  now  the   state ly  -mov ing  Ple   ia   des,

     —    /    —     /    —    /    —     /     —    /
5    In   that soft  in   finite dark ness o     ver  head

     —    /    —     /    —    /    —     /     —    /
6    Hang jew  el    -wise up   on  a    sil   ver  thread.
```

Notice that line 3 begins with a trochee, not an iamb. Iambic pentameter is very forgiving of slight variations. In fact, poets often add slight variations deliberately to avoid monotony. Nevertheless, this poem is written in iambic pentameter because that is the most common meter. Also notice that line 5, *infinite* is best pronounced as though it has only two syllables. This preserves the most common meter and the number of syllables per line.

The regularity of the rhyme scheme and the regular number of syllables in each line match the regular movement of the stars in the night sky.

Understand the Poem as a Whole

At this point, the work of understanding the poem should be a matter of summarizing the main points of the analysis. The poem is a **lyric**, a short poem that expresses the emotions or thoughts of the writer. The first stanza describes the night sky and the second stanza describes the poet's thoughts about life. Both stanzas express her emotions.

Does this summary of the poem seem flat compared to the poem itself? It should. What would be the point of poetry if thoughts and emotions could be satisfactorily communicated in a few lines of textbook prose? Why would poets bother to work with imagery, figures of speech, sound, rhythm, rhyme, and all the rest if they could express themselves in simpler ways? In fact, ordinary language cannot contain all that we experience of life. That is why poetry is written.

Free Verse and Rhythm

Free verse also contains rhythm, although it is not as regular. Here is a short poem by Walt Whitman. Try reading it aloud. Notice the definite, but irregular rhythm. This kind of rhythm is sometimes called cadence, and it is closer to ordinary speech than the regular rhythms of metrical verse.

> ## WHEN I HEARD THE LEARN'D ASTRONOMER
>
> When I heard the learn'd astronomer,
> When the proofs, the figures, were ranged in columns before me,
> When I was shown the charts and diagrams, to add, divide, and measure them,
> When I sitting heard the astronomer where he lectured with much applause in the lecture-room,
>
> How soon unaccountable I became tired and sick,
> Till rising and gliding out I wander'd off by myself,
> In the mystical moist night-air, and from time to time,
> Look'd up in perfect silence at the stars.
>
> —*by* Walt Whitman

Notice how Whitman turns the two-syllable *learned* into the one-syllable *learn'd*. (When *learned* is used as an adjective, it is pronounced with two syllables: *learn-ed*. Whitman's *learn'd* is pronounced like the verb.) In writing free verse, he is just as careful with rhythm as a poet writing metrical verse, only his rhythms are different. When reading free verse, students should read with the rhythm and listen to how it contributes to the poet's intention. In this example, lines 3–5 are long and written with a repetitive rhythm that echoes Whitman's boredom and dislike. The rhythms of the concluding lines change as he escapes from the lecture-room.

KINDS OF POETRY

THE SONNET

The sonnet is a complex form that has been popular for centuries. **Sonnets** are lyric poems fourteen lines long, and when written in English, usually iambic pentameter. The **Elizabethan**, or **Shakespearean** sonnet consists of three **quatrains** (four-line stanzas) and a **couplet** (two lines) all written to a strict **end-rhyme scheme** (*abab cdcd efef gg*). The development of the poet's thoughts is also structured. There are several methods. One method is to use each quatrain for different points in an argument and the couplet for the resolution of the argument. Because of the complexity of the sonnet, poets sometimes find it a suitable form for expressing the complexity of thought and emotion.

GENRE

Lyric	A short poem that expresses the emotions or thoughts of the writer. Sonnets, odes, and elegies are examples of lyrics. *Lyrics* are the words of a song. A song, of course, is often a lyric in the first sense.
Ode	A poem expressing lofty emotion. Odes often celebrate an event, or are addressed to nature or to some person, place, or thing. An example is "Ode to a Grecian Urn" by John Keats.
Ballad	A narrative poem that tells a story, often in a straightforward and dramatic manner, and often about such universals as love, honour, and courage. Ballads were once songs, and literary ballads often have the strong rhythm and plain rhymes of songs. Songs are still written in ballad form; some old ballads are still sung; and, some literary ballads have been set to music. Samuel Taylor Coleridge's "The Rime of the Ancient Mariner" is an example of a literary ballad. "The Mary Ellen Carter" by Stan Rogers is an example of a modern song-ballad.
Epic	A long poem that is often about a heroic character. The style is elevated and the poetry often represents religious, or cultural ideals. The Iliad and the Odyssey are examples of epics.

Each of these kinds of poems could be written as free verse or in any of the traditional meters.

Copyright Protected

POETIC DEVICES

Poetic devices are the tools that poets use to convey emotion and meaning. Here are some of the more common devices.

Alliteration	The repetition of initial consonants, as in this quotation from *Beowulf*: *Lo, praise of the prowess of people-kings / of spear-armed Danes, in days long sped...*
Assonance	Like rhyme, but only the repeated vowels are the same or almost the same. (*load, loan*; *mess, lend*). Another kind of assonance is called half rhyme. Consonants match, but vowels do not (*tin, tan*; *stake, stick*). Some poems use half rhyme in place of full rhyme.
Dissonance	The use of discordant or unpleasant sounds
Onomatopoeia	The use of words that suggest the sound of the thing they describe. Tennyson's *murmuring of innumerable bees* imitates the sound of bees through the use of assonance.
Rhyme	The repetition of the same sounds. Syllables, entire words, or groups of words can rhyme. As a rule, rhyme consists of the last stressed vowel and all the sounds after it. (*infernal, eternal*; *laughter, rafter*; *ring high*; *sing high*). Rhyme is usually found at the end of a line of poetry, but sometimes it occurs within the line (internal rhyme).
Simile	A comparison using like or as: *an eager spirit like a bright flame*
Metaphor	A direct comparison: *his eager spirit a bright flame.*
Apostrophe	A figure of speech addressed to someone who is dead or absent, or to an inanimate object. E.g., *Milton! thou shouldst be living at this hour.* (Wordsworth) See personification. Do not confuse this apostrophe with the punctuation mark (').
Metonymy	A figure of speech that uses an attribute of a thing or something associated with the thing to stand for the thing itself e.g., *The **suits** make the decisions around here.*
Synecdoche	Like metonymy except that a part of something is used to stand for the whole thing. e.g., *Many **hands** make light work.*
Personification	The attribution of human characteristics to non-human things. Shakespeare's *Blow, blow, thou winter wind, / Thou art not so unkind / As man's ingratitude; / Thy tooth is not so keen* contains both an apostrophe and personification.
Symbolism	The use of one thing to represent something else. Although symbolism is similar to metonymy, the association may be arbitrary. For example, Canada is often symbolized by maple leaves, as on our flag. A maple leaf has nothing to do with Canada as a country, and the maple tree grows in many countries. The symbolism may be invented by the author.

Not for Reproduction

Read poetic language with careful attention. For example, the phrase *leaves whispering* may be intended **literally**, for trees in a poem may be aware and have the power of speech. However, the words are more likely meant **figuratively**. Then how are they to be understood? A metaphor or personification like *leaves whispering* can have several functions.

- It can describe the sound of moving leaves by comparing them to whispering.

- It can also describe something else, perhaps a voice, by comparing it to the sound of moving leaves. For example, a small voice like dry leaves whispering.

- The same figure of speech can be used to suggest something other than just sound. For example, the whispering leaves could represent nature communicating secrets impossible to hear.

In the last case, the metaphor would be an important part of the poet's thought and it might be developed at length, or it might appear again in other parts of the poem. An extended metaphor, especially if it is elaborate, is called a **conceit**.

WRITING ESSAYS

An Essay Template

Many students find essay writing very challenging. This is partly because they do not realize that there is a pattern to the basic essay, and that the pattern can be easily learned and applied.

This pattern is based on graphic organizers. It is intended to be a starting point for most of the essays that you will have to write. You should alter the basic pattern to suit your own abilities and tastes.

Begin with the familiar **hamburger paragraph**, which looks like this:

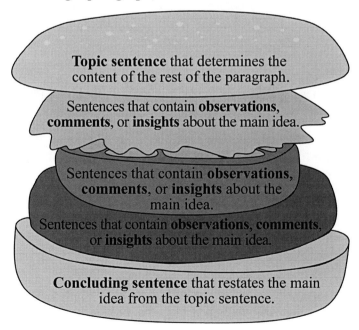

Not all paragraphs start with a topic sentence. There are other patterns of organization. However, this is the basic, one-size-fits-all paragraph that works in most situations.

Now think of the essay as an extension of the hamburger paragraph. Here is picture of the hamburger essay:

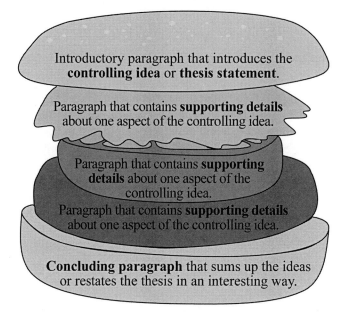

Not all essays follow this pattern. Again, this is the basic, one-size-fits-all essay that works in most situations. This is the pattern that is frequently required of students.

These graphic organizers each contain an opening, a closing, and three items in between. This does not mean that you are limited to three body sentences in a paragraph and three body paragraphs in an essay. However, the five-paragraph essay is very common.

THE THESIS STATEMENT

It is not absolutely necessary to include a thesis statement in the first paragraph; in fact, it is not always necessary to actually state a thesis. Sometimes a thesis is implied. However, many teachers like to see the thesis statement written clearly in the first paragraph.

The thesis is the same thing as the theme of the essay. The **thesis** is made up of a topic and a point of view. It is often called the **controlling idea** because it is the idea that controls the selection of all the other ideas included in the essay.

Thesis = Theme = Controlling idea

A **thesis statement** is a sentence that expresses the thesis. The thesis statement includes the topic and what will be said about the topic.

Macbeth + is destroyed by his ambition = Thesis statement

The thesis statement is most often a single sentence, but may be more.

Copyright Protected

The hamburger paragraph can be used to include the thesis statement. Here is a template for the first paragraph.

1	Write a topic sentence that introduces the topic itself.
2	Write several sentences that explain the topic.
3	Write a thesis statement that restates the topic and tells what position you will be taking.

TRANSITIONAL DEVICES

Transitional devices are words and phrases like *because*, *also*, *in addition*, *nevertheless*, and *as a result*. These words show the relationship between ideas.

- *In addition*, the witness has already admitted to lying. *Therefore*, you must consider whether or not any of her evidence can be believed. *On the other hand*, other witnesses have confirmed some of her statements.

Careful writers use transitional devices to make the relationships between the parts of an essay clear. Transitional devices can be used to show a sequence or to begin a paragraph by showing how the ideas in the paragraph are related to the ideas in the preceding paragraph.

- As you consider the evidence, you will have to keep in mind the fact that the witness has admitted to lying on three occasions.

- *First, … Next, … And finally, …*

- *On the other hand*, her evidence about the escape vehicle has been confirmed by …

- *Therefore*, you will have to decide how much weight to give to her statements about …

- *To conclude*, it seems that we can agree …

DETECTING LOGICAL FALLACIES

Essays are often meant to persuade. Sometimes persuasion is based on appeals to emotion, but the only lasting persuasion is based on facts and reason. Facts can be difficult to check, but the logical presentation of facts can be checked by anyone who is prepared to pay attention to detail and to use common sense.

You must know some history to understand that the following sentence is nonsense.

- Once Grand Duchess Amelia had been crowned queen-empress of Transylvania, she immediately began to plot the invasion of France.

However, students can easily see that the following is nonsense.

- Well of course he's crooked. He's a politician, isn't he? And we know what politicians are like.

A moment's thought makes it clear that there is no way that anything can be concluded about a person's honesty from the mere fact that he or she is a politician. It is easy to see the error in thought if the statements are rearranged and written in the form of a syllogism:

All politicians are corrupt.	Major premise	All P are C
He is a politician.	Minor premise	X is P
He is corrupt.	Conclusion	X is C

Copyright Protected

You can see that the conclusion follows, but *only if both premises are true*. In other words, the argument is valid, *but only if all politicians are corrupt*. How can anyone possibly know that for a fact? We know enough about human nature to doubt that premise. There is no reason why any individual might not be honest. Simply taking up a certain profession does not automatically produce corruption.

Syllogisms allow us to examine statements and decide if the logical connections between them are valid. Although you cannot check matters of fact with a syllogism, you can check matters of logic. Then you can easily discover the facts that you will have to check through investigation. Here is an example.

- Recently, a wild game farm was closed after it was discovered that the animals on the farm were starving. An animal rights activist was interviewed on television and said, among other things, "This is the second time this has happened. Enough is enough. This is a failed experiment and the government must shut down all wild game farms."

The activist might have been right or he might have been wrong, but his argument was inadequate.
He said two things:

1	• More than one failed game farm shows that all game farms have failed.
	• Two game farms have failed.
	• All game farms are a failure.
2	• If all game farms are a failure, they should be closed.
	• All game farms are a failure.
	• All game farms should be closed.

The activist's conclusions would follow, *but only if his premises were true*. Of course, there is no way of knowing that. The premises might be true, or they might not be. Further investigation would be required.

Sometimes the syllogism itself is invalid. In this example, the conclusion does not follow from the premises.

All mammals are warm-blooded.	Major premise	All M are W
Birds are not mammals	Minor premise	B are not M
Birds are not warm-blooded.	Conclusion	B are not W

This argument is invalid. The major premise is about M and W, the conclusion is about B and W, but the minor premise is about B and M. There is nothing to connect B and W.

The conclusion is also false. It is already known that birds are warm-blooded.

Use syllogisms to analyze arguments.

Remember that syllogisms cannot be used to check matters of fact.

If a premise is false, then the conclusion does not follow, *but that conclusion might still be a true statement*. It is just that the argument needs to be improved.

Remember that if an argument is invalid, then the conclusion does not follow, *but that conclusion might still be a true statement*. It is just that the argument needs to be improved.

WRITING MECHANICS

PARTS OF SPEECH

Nouns are the names of persons, places, or things. Capitalize proper nouns. Nouns include these types:

- **Countable** nouns like *marbles*, *trees*, and *stars* can be counted and may be singular or plural.
- **Uncountable** nouns like *maturity*, *intelligence*, and *courage* cannot be counted and are singular.
- Nouns like *water*, *sand*, and *grain* are countable or uncountable depending on their use.
- **Collective** nouns like *committee*, *staff*, *family*, *crowd*, and *class* are singular unless there is a particular reason to treat them as plural.
- **Nominals** are words or phrases used as nouns. *Skiing*, *watching paint dry*, and *to go long distance running* are not nouns, but they could be used as nouns in some sentences.
- **Appositives** are words or phrases that rename a noun. *My friend Jack will be there. Jack*, an appositive, renames *friend*.

Pronouns take the place of nouns.

- The **antecedent** of a pronoun is the noun that the pronoun stands for. In the phrase *Goneril demanded that she be first*, the antecedent of the word *she* is *Goneril*.
- **Indefinite** pronouns like *another*, *anybody*, *somebody*, *nobody*, and *none* are generally singular.

Adjectives modify or describe nouns and pronouns. Capitalize proper adjectives unless long use has made them common. (*Canadian*, *Parisian*, but *italic* (script), *gothic* (novel), *zeppelin*)

- **Adjectivals** are any word or group of words that act as adjectives.
- The **articles**, *a*, *an*, and *the* are considered adjectives.

Verbs usually name actions such as *laugh*, *sleep*, *think*.

- Most English verbs are **regular**; that is, their past tense and past participle forms end in *-ed*. There are about three hundred **irregular** verbs. The appendices section contains lists of irregular verbs.
- **Transitive** verbs have a direct object. They do something to the object. In the phrase *The ball struck the batter*, *batter* is the direct object of the word *struck*.
- **Intransitive** verbs do not have direct objects. The verbs *lie* (to tell a lie) and *arrive* are intransitive. You cannot *arrive* anything, or *lie* anything.
- Most verbs are transitive or intransitive depending on how they are used.
  - transitive: *He produced a sheaf of papers.*
  - intransitive: *When irrigated, the wasteland produced abundantly.*
- **Linking** verbs like *be*, *taste*, *look*, and *sound* describe states of being. Other linking verbs like *turn*, *become*, and *grow* describe changes in state. Remember that linking verbs are usually followed by nouns or adjectives, that is, nominals or adjectivals.
  - She *is a* lawyer.
  - This milk *tastes* sour.

Copyright Protected

Adverbs modify or describe a verb, an adjective, or another adverb.

- She ran *quickly*.
- His closely reasoned argument was *brilliant*.
- They worked *very* hard.

Adverbials are any word or group of words that act as an adverb.

- *After the long, hard day*, we went fishing.
- Adverbs and adverbials describe *when*, *where*, *how*, *why*, and *how much*.
  - You can rest *later*.
  - She went *somewhere* over the rainbow.
  - They shuffled their feet *nervously*.
  - *Because he was sick*, he fell down.

Prepositions are words placed in front of nouns and pronouns to create a phrase.

- *for* a cause
- *by* them
- Together with the noun or pronoun, prepositions link phrases to some other word in the sentence.
  - They worked *for a cause*. *For a cause* is an adverbial prepositional phrase modifying worked.
  - The child *by them* shouted. *By them* is an adjectival prepositional phrase modifying child.
- **Prepositional phrases** are usually adjectivals or adverbials.

Conjunctions join words, phrases, clauses, and sentences. They also show the relationship between the things that are joined. They show whether the things joined are equal or unequal.

- Conjunctions connect both sentences and sentence parts.
- **Coordinating conjunctions** like *and*, *so*, and *or* join equal parts.
  - Sir Toby likes cakes *and* ale.
  - You must lead *or* follow.
  - Chopping firewood *and* painting the trim are next.
  - We went to the wedding, *and* we went to the reception.
- **Correlative** conjunctions like either-or and neither-nor join equal parts.
  - Malvolio likes *neither* cakes *nor* ale.
  - You must *either* lead *or* follow.
  - *Either* you must chop firewood, *or* you must paint the trim.
- **Subordinating** conjunctions like *whenever* and *however* join unequal parts.
  - *Whenever* I hear that song, I want to laugh.
  - You must be careful *whenever* you cross the street.
  - *However* you arrange it, be sure that you are back by Tuesday.

Interjections express some form of emotion.

- *Ouch*! That hurts.
- *Oh*, I don't know.

THE SENTENCE

A sentence is made up of a **subject** (the minimum subject is a noun) and a **predicate** (the minimum predicate is a verb). When proofreading and editing, it is often necessary to focus on the minimum subject and predicate.

Subject			Predicate		
Nominal	+	Everything attached to the nominal	Verb	+	Everything attached to the verb
Birds			*fly.*		
The *suspects*			*are* the ones.		
The five *suspects* that you see before you this morning			*are* certainly the ones who raided the fridge during the night.		

Sometimes the subject comes after the predicate.

Predicate	Subject
Down the mountainside *thundered*	the *avalanche*.

SENTENCE FAULTS

Lack of Agreement Among Parts of a Sentence

Subject and Verb

The basic rule of subject-verb agreement should not cause any difficulty.

- It is ready.
- They are ready.
- Sampson and Delilah are not friends any more.

Most of the difficulties in subject-verb agreement are caused by difficulties in recognizing singular and plural subjects.

- When subjects are joined by the words *or* or *nor*, the verb agrees with the nearest subject.
  - Either Miller *or* Smith *is* guilty.
  - Neither Miller *nor* Smith *wants* to confess.
  - Neither the speaker *nor* the listeners *are* aware of the irony.

Copyright Protected

- When one part of the subject is singular, and the other plural, write the sentence so that the plural part is nearest the verb.
  - Weak: Neither *band members* nor the ***conductor is*** satisfied.
  - Better: Neither the *conductor* nor the ***band members are*** satisfied.
- Nothing that comes between a singular subject and its verb can make that subject plural. Students should not make the verb agree with the nearest noun.
  - Our school basketball *team*, the Gerbils, **is** victorious again.
  - The *prime minister*, accompanied by several cabinet ministers, *arrives* at the airport shortly.
  - Either *Miller* or *Jones*—both are suspects—*is* guilty.
  - The *contestant* with the most votes **is** now on the stage.
  - *One* of the girls *sings* better.
  - The *ringleader* who was at the head of the rebellious miners *is* sorry.
- Indefinite pronouns like *each, each one, either, neither, everyone, everybody, anybody, anyone, nobody, somebody, someone,* and *no one* are singular.
  - *Each* of the contestants *wins* a prize.
  - *Everybody* near the river *is* in danger.
  - *No one* who wants to be successful in these exams *is* likely to be late.
- Collective nouns are singular unless there is a reason to consider them as plurals.
  - The *group works* well.
  - The *company is* bankrupt.
  - The *jury is* deliberating its verdict.
  - The *jury are* arguing among *themselves.*

The Wrong Pronoun

Using the correct pronoun is often a problem because the form of a pronoun varies depending on how the pronoun is used.

- Use *I, you, he/she/it, we, you, they, who,* as the subject of a sentence or clause, and for the complement of a linking verb
  - *You* have been chosen.
  - *We* will be the last of the contestants.
  - *Who* is going to be next?
  - It is *she* who will be chosen.

Not for Reproduction

- Use *me, you, him/her/it, us, you, them*, and *whom* as direct or indirect objects of verbs or as the object of a preposition
  - Give it to *me*.
  - Hit the ball to *them*.
  - Ask *them* the time.
  - The child next to *him* laughed suddenly.
- Use *my, your, his/her/its, our, your, their*, and *whose* as adjectives.
  - *My* car
  - *Your* umbrella
  - *Its* fur
- Use *mine, yours, his/hers/its, ours, yours, theirs*, and *whose* as subjects of sentences or as the complement of a linking verb
  - *Yours* is the one on the left.
  - This is *mine*.
  - *Theirs* is next.

The possessive pronouns *my, your, his, hers, its, our, yours, theirs*, and *whose* **never** use an apostrophe to show possession.

Fragments, Comma Splices, and Run-ons

As a general rule, all sentences should be complete sentences.

- Incorrect: He went ahead with his plan. <u>Even though it was faulty.</u>
- Correct: He went ahead with his plan, even though it was faulty.

Occasionally, an incomplete sentence is used deliberately for effect. Fragments that are used deliberately are sometimes called minor sentences.

- Correct: Is anyone is in favour of dictatorship? <u>No</u>? <u>Well, of course not.</u>

Dialogue and reported speech are exceptions to the rule about fragments.

- "Ready yet?"
  "Not yet."
  "Well then—!"

The opposite error is the "sentence" that is really two sentences. Either punctuation between sentences is omitted, or a comma is used to join two sentences.

- Run-on: We went to Calgary we decided to visit Banff.
- Comma splice: We went to Calgary, we decided to visit Banff.

These errors can be fixed by correcting the punctuation or by rewriting.

- We went to Calgary. We decided to visit Banff.
- We went to Calgary. Then we decided to visit Banff.
- After we went to Calgary, we decided to visit Banff.
- We went to Calgary; then we decided to visit Banff.

Copyright Protected

PUNCTUATION

Periods

The period is used at the end of most sentences and after fragments that are deliberately used as sentences.

- I walked to the end of the world. And stared.

Do not use a period after a complete sentence that is contained by parentheses within another sentence.

- Afghanistan is making progress (seven thousand technicians have been trained) and will one day finish the job of clearing mines.

Punctuating Possessives

Most possessives are formed by adding an apostrophe and an *s*.

- A girl's smile
- One country's history

The possessive of nouns ending in an *s* sound is formed by adding an apostrophe and an *s*.

- The boss's car
- Charles's, Alex's

The possessive of plurals is formed by adding an apostrophe after the *s* of the plural.

- Five girls' smiles
- Three countries' histories

Commas

Commas With Conjunctions

Coordinating conjunctions are used to join complete sentences. They are usually followed by a comma. The coordinating conjunctions are *for*, *and*, *nor*, *but*, *or*, *yet*, and *so*. They may be remembered by remembering the mnemonic FANBOYS.

- He will be late, for he must complete the game.
- Go to the edge of the cliff, and tell me what you see there.

However, when a coordinate conjunction joins two short independent clauses, a comma may not be necessary.

- She's late and she's tired.

When **subordinating conjunctions** (which include *after*, *because*, *although*, *if*, *before*, *since*, *though*, and *unless*) are used in an introductory clause, a comma follows the clause.

- Because you have been elected, you must serve.
- Before she leaves, she plans to write a note of farewell.

Do not use a semicolon to follow an introductory clause.

- Incorrect: Because you have been elected; you must serve.

When the subordinate clause follows the independent clause, a comma is usually not used.

- She plans to write a note of farewell before she leaves.
- You must serve because you have been elected.

However, a comma should be used when it is necessary to avoid confusion.

- Unclear: He has done all his work since his failure last term threatened his final grade.
- Clear: He has done all his work, since his failure last term threatened his final grade.

Until near the end, the original sentence seems to mean that he has done all his work from the time that his failure threatened his final grade. A comma after *work* makes it clear that *since* is a subordinating conjunction meaning *because*, not a preposition.

Commas With Introductory Phrases

Some introductory phrases have been previously mentioned. Other kinds of introductory phrases are also followed by a comma.

- During the long summer afternoon, we were able to catch up on our work.
- Knowing he was beaten, he conceded defeat.
- Near a small clump of trees, we made our camp.
- Running out of money, he cabled home for more.
- In addition, we will need rope and flashlights.

When a **conjunctive adverb** (an adverb used as a conjunction) is used after a semicolon, it is still an introductory element.

- He had failed his entrance examination; moreover, he had not submitted his papers.

Sometimes a conjunctive adverb does not require a comma. A comma would interrupt the flow of a sentence like the following.

- Then we decided to visit Banff.

The Serial Comma

Use a comma after all the items in a series.

- Bring food, extra clothing, a first aid kit, and matches.
- A dictionary, a thesaurus, and a writing guide may be used for the English 30-1 and 30-2 final writing examinations.

A semicolon should be used after each item in the series when the items already include commas.

- The men endured a long, hot march; flies, dust, and brackish water; and a raging, howling sandstorm.

Copyright Protected

Setting Off Appositives

Appositives, or restatements of a **nominal** (a noun or a word or phrase used as a noun) are set off by commas.

- Our team, the Hornets, is in first place.
- His American cousins, the Sinclairs, were all present at the reunion.
- Everyone in Calgary, the home of the Flames hockey team, is watching the Stanley Cup playoffs.

However, when the appositive is used to distinguish something that belongs to a larger group of similar things, no comma is used.

- The poem "Stars" was written by Marjorie Pickthall.
- The Tribal class destroyer *HMCS Athabaskan* was sunk in 1944.

Notice that *HMCS Athabaskan* cannot rename the noun phrase "Tribal class destroyer" as there were many other ships in that class, or group. This is an example of a rule explained more fully in the following section.

Setting Off Nonessential Clauses

Clauses are word groups containing a subject and a verb. Sentences are independent clauses. Dependent or subordinate clauses can be part of a sentence. **Nonessential clauses**, which are also called **non-restrictive clauses**, can be removed from a sentence without altering the essential meaning of the sentence. They merely add extra information. Set off nonessential clauses with commas.

- Her car, which she had painted red, is in the shop again.
- Her car needs a new transmission, which will be expensive.

Essential clauses cannot be removed from a sentence without changing the meaning of the sentence. They restrict the meaning of a sentence, and are sometimes called **restrictive clauses**.

- The car that she needs for work is in the shop again. (In other words, one particular car is in the shop.)

Commas can be used to make a clause essential or non-essential and thus alter the meaning of a sentence.

- His uncle, who lives in New York, saw the World Trade Towers collapse. (His uncle saw the collapse. The uncle also happens to live in New York.)
- His uncle who lives in New York saw the World Trade Towers collapse. (One particular uncle saw the collapse. But his other uncles, who live in other cities, did not.)

Notice that *which* is used with non-essential or non-restrictive clauses. *That* is used with essential or restrictive clauses. *Who* is usually used when referring to persons.

Commas With Adjectives

When more than one adjective appear in front of a noun, commas are sometimes necessary.

- Fierce, tough dogs,
  but
- Three fierce, tough dogs,
  and
- Three fierce, tough old dogs,
  and
- Three fierce old sheep dogs

Do not put a comma between **cumulative adjectives**, or adjectives that build on each other to modify a noun. Each adjective modifies the noun and adjective group that follows it.

- Four vile yellow plastic figurines
- Her beautiful old Georgian town house

Cumulative adjectives have a certain order; they cannot be switched around.

- Incorrect: vile four plastic yellow figurines
- Incorrect: beautiful her Georgian town old house

In addition, cumulative adjectives cannot be written using the word *and*.

- Incorrect: vile and four and plastic figurines

The order cannot be changed because there is a conventional order of cumulative adjectives. There are sometimes variations, but this is the most common order.

Article, Possessive, Number	Observation, Judgement, Evaluation, Opinion	Physical Description					Place of Origin, Source	Material, What It Is Made of	Qualifier, Type, Class	Noun
		Size	Shape	Condition	Age	Colour				
several	handsome	big	square	worn	old	red	Italian	leather	running	shoes

Place a comma between **coordinate adjectives**, or adjectives that modify a noun independently. These are often the same kind of adjective.

- A soft, gentle breeze
- A harsh, rigid, inflexible critic

Copyright Protected

The order of coordinate adjectives can be changed.

- A gentle, soft breeze
- A rigid, harsh, inflexible critic

Notice that *inflexible*, which is used here as an observation or evaluation adjective, is also a physical description adjective. As a result, it "sounds" a little better when it is written in the order it would follow if it were used as a cumulative adjective describing physical condition.

Coordinate adjectives can also be written using the word *and*.

- a soft and gentle breeze
- a rigid and harsh and inflexible critic

Colons in Sentences

When used in sentences, a colon must follow an independent clause. It introduces a list, an explanation, or an appositive (a word or phrase that restates a noun).

- You should bring the following items: a sleeping bag, a change of clothes, and matches.
- There is only one honest thing to do: admit you made a mistake and apologize.
- His character was summed up in his name: Gradgrind.

The list may be set up in point form. The same rule applies.

- The introductory course will cover three topics:
  1. algebra
  2. geometry
  3. trigonometry

If a list does not follow an independent clause (a complete sentence) no colon is used.

- You must bring a sleeping bag, a change of clothes, and matches.
- The introductory course will cover
  1. algebra
  2. geometry
  3. trigonometry

A simple way of checking colon use is to cover up all the words after the colon. Can the first part of the sentence now stand alone as a sentence? If not, then do not use the colon.

- Incorrect: You must bring: a sleeping bag, a change of clothes, and matches.
- Correct: You must bring the following items: a sleeping bag, a change of clothes, and matches.

Quotation Marks

Use quotation marks at the beginning and end of all words in a **direct quotation** (someone's exact words). Watch for the use of quotes before and after a **speech tag**. Also notice the use of the comma after the speech tag ("Alfred said") as in the first example.

- Alfred said, "We are ready."
- "I'm finished the job," said Alfred. "We can go now."
- "When we are ready," said Alfred, "we will go."

Also notice that the closing quotation mark is placed after a comma or a period.

Closing quotation marks are also used with exclamation marks and question marks. When these punctuation marks belong to the sentence, they are placed outside the closing quotation marks.

- Didn't you hear him say, "I'm in trouble"?

If the question mark belongs to the quotation, it is placed inside the quotation marks.

- He said sadly, "Why is it always me?"

The same rules apply to end punctuation used for other purposes. Periods and commas belong inside the quotation marks. Exclamation and question marks belong either outside or inside the quotation marks, depending on whether they belong to the sentence as a whole or to the words inside the quotation marks.

- You could say that her acting was "over the top."
- I can't believe that's your "best effort"!

Indirect quotations, or quotations that do not repeat exact words, never require quotation marks.

- Alfred asked if we were ready.
- Alfred said that he had finished the job and that we could go.

Quotation marks are also used set off the titles of short stories and poems.

- Marjorie Pickthall wrote "Stars."

Quotation marks indicate that a word is being used in an unusual sense.

- "Housekeeping" on the space station is challenging.

Quotation marks can also show that a word is used **ironically**. When a word is used ironically, it has a meaning opposite to its literal meaning.

- The "suicide" of Jan Masaryk marked the end of democracy in Czechoslovakia.
- It seems that your "help" has put this project three weeks behind.

READING FOR EXAMINATIONS

When you are reading for an examination, or for any important purpose, you cannot read casually. An overview, a general idea, or a skimming of the main ideas rarely gives the best results. Instead, a **close reading**, a careful examination of everything in a text, is required.

CLOSE READING

Close reading is like the method of unpacking a poem. (See the "Reading Poetry" section.) It begins with careful attention to the meanings of words and ends with considering the meaning of the entire work.

Close reading is examining the different levels of meaning.

Meanings of words and sentences	• The basic level of understanding is understanding the meanings of words. A dictionary may be needed, but on an exam a dictionary is not available. • Use context clues to figure out or to approximate the meanings of unfamiliar words.
Meanings of images, symbols, references, allusions	• These literary devices are mostly indirect (references are an exception) but they are important to meaning and must be considered carefully.
Writing techniques	• The most important part of a sentence is often placed first. • The subject of an essay is often stated in the opening paragraph and restated in the last paragraph. The topic of a paragraph is often stated in the first sentence and restated in the last sentence. • Transitional devices guide the development of ideas and show the relationships between ideas. • Narratives often follow the structure shown in the plot diagram and contain the elements of narrative described earlier.
The writer's meaning	• The controlling idea, or the theme, or the thesis controls everything from the form and genre to the choice of words. Consider everything in relation to the controlling idea.

The multiple choice questions also require close reading.

It is just as important to understand the question as it is to understand the text that the question is testing. For example, here is one of the questions from the first reading in the first sample exam at the end of this *KEY*.

1. The reason why the new Globe is so famous could be **best** described as
    A. it faithfully reproduces so many aspects of the original Globe
    B. it has received favourable reviews in the media
    C. it has mounted many of Shakespeare's most popular plays
    D. Shakespearean drama is timeless

Questions that contain words like *best, most accurately*, or *most completely* are **evaluation questions**. All the responses are correct to some degree. You will need to read the entire question and the relevant part of the text carefully. Then you will be able to choose the *best, most accurate*, or *most complete* answer.

Apply Your Knowledge of Form and Genre

As soon as you see that you are about to read an essay, you know that you will likely find an introductory paragraph and a concluding paragraph. It is often useful to read these first. You will also expect to find transitional devices used throughout. You will want to pay special attention to these devices, perhaps underlining or highlighting them.

On the other hand, a story might be best read in order. At the same time, you might want to sketch a plot diagram or note characterization, setting, and theme.

On an exam, circle or underline important words in the instructions, readings, and questions.

Context Clues

You should always pay attention to context. Here is an example that shows why. Consider the following question.

2. In the context of lines 5–8, anxious means

    A. eager

    B. worried

    C. doubtful

    D. uncertain

You might take one look, and choose *worried* because anxious does mean worried. The other responses are obviously incorrect but the question refers to lines 5 to 8. *What does the word mean in context?* Let us say that you read lines 5 to 8 and find

> Premier Jones is anxious to read the results of the Cottonwood Developments enquiry as soon as it is available.

Worried does not fit in the context of the sentence. Worried to read? That cannot be right. Worried is not used with the preposition *to*.

The only word that fits is *eager*. Strictly speaking, such a use is incorrect, but it is common in informal language.

How could you be sure that *anxious* is used to mean *eager*? After all, the word really means *worried*. When you are not sure, read more of the context. Perhaps you might find something like the following.

> Insider information indicates that the report will completely clear the government of all wrongdoing.

Now the context of the situation makes the meaning even clearer. Premier Jones would not be worried when the report will clear the government. Instead, the premier would be eager to read the report.

Always pay close attention to context.

Copyright Protected

IRONY AND LEVELS OF MEANING

Students often do poorly when the surface meaning of a text is not the real meaning. Consider the following example.

- It seems that your "help" has put this project three weeks behind.

In this case, the quotation marks indicate that the word *help* is meant ironically. **Irony** is the use of words to express something other than the literal meaning. In the next example Jane Austen is using irony for humorous effect in the opening sentences of *Pride and Prejudice*.

- "It is a truth universally acknowledged that a single man in possession of a good fortune must be in want of a wife."

When the irony is intended to hurt, and especially when it is accompanied by a cutting tone of voice (or sometimes by quotation marks, as above), it is called **sarcasm**.

In **verbal irony**, it is the words that have the opposite of their intended meaning. In **situational irony**, there is either a difference between appearance and reality or a difference between what happens and what is expected to happen.

- It would be ironic if someone died in a car accident on the way to pick up a million dollar lottery win.
- Irony also exists when a politician defends the rule of law when she is secretly breaking the law.

The last example is also an example of **hypocrisy**, or doing one thing while saying another.

Dramatic irony and **tragic irony** are forms of situational irony found in literature. The irony exists when the audience knows something that the characters do not know. Sometimes other characters also know what the audience knows.

- When King Duncan arrives at Macbeth's castle, he is greeted with a display of hospitality and friendliness. This an example of tragic irony because in the previous scene, Macbeth and Lady Macbeth plotted to murder their king.

Watch for irony of situation or of words. Sometimes the surface meaning is not the real meaning. You should expect questions that test your ability to recognize irony.

KEY Strategies for Success on Tests

Copyright Protected

KEY STRATEGIES FOR SUCCESS ON TESTS

THINGS TO CONSIDER WHEN TAKING A TEST

It is normal to feel anxious before you write a test. You can manage this anxiety by using the following strategies:

- Think positive thoughts. Imagine yourself doing well on the test.

- Make a conscious effort to relax by taking several slow, deep, controlled breaths. Concentrate on the air going in and out of your body.

- Before you begin the test, ask questions if you are unsure of anything.

- Jot down key words or phrases from any instructions your teacher gives you.

- Look over the entire test to find out the number and kinds of questions on the test.

- Read each question closely, and reread if necessary.

- Pay close attention to key vocabulary words. Sometimes, these words are **bolded** or *italicized*, and they are usually important words in the question.

- If you are putting your answers on an answer sheet, mark your answers carefully. Always print clearly. If you wish to change an answer, erase the mark completely, and ensure that your final answer is darker than the one you have erased.

- Use highlighting to note directions, key words, and vocabulary that you find confusing or that are important to answering the question.

- Double-check to make sure you have answered everything before handing in your test.

- When taking tests, students often overlook the easy words. Failure to pay close attention to these words can result in an incorrect answer. One way to avoid this is to be aware of these words and to underline, circle, or highlight them while you are taking the test.

- Even though some words are easy to understand, they can change the meaning of the entire question, so it is important that you pay attention to them. Here are some examples.

all	always	most likely	probably	best	not
difference	usually	except	most	unlikely	likely

Example

1. Which of the following expressions is **incorrect**?

   A. $3 + 2 \geq 5$

   B. $4 - 3 < 2$

   C. $5 \times 4 < 15$

   D. $6 \times 3 \geq 18$

Not for Reproduction

TEST PREPARATION AND TEST-TAKING SKILLS

HELPFUL STRATEGIES FOR ANSWERING MULTIPLE-CHOICE QUESTIONS

A multiple-choice question gives you some information and then asks you to select an answer from four choices. Each question has one correct answer. The other choices are distractors, which are incorrect.

The following strategies can help you when answering multiple-choice questions:

- Quickly skim through the entire test. Find out how many questions there are, and plan your time accordingly.

- Read and reread questions carefully. Underline key words, and try to think of an answer before looking at the choices.

- If there is a graphic, look at the graphic, read the question, and go back to the graphic. Then, you may want to underline the important information from the question.

- Carefully read the choices. Read the question first and then each choice that goes with it.

- When choosing an answer, try to eliminate those choices that are clearly wrong or do not make sense.

- Some questions may ask you to select the best answer. These questions will always include words like *best*, *most appropriate*, or *most likely*. All of the choices will be correct to some degree, but one of the choices will be better than the others in some way. Carefully read all four choices before choosing the answer you think is the best.

- If you do not know the answer, or if the question does not make sense to you, it is better to guess than to leave it blank.

- Do not spend too much time on any one question. Make a mark (*) beside a difficult question, and come back to it later. If you are leaving a question to come back to later, make sure you also leave the space on the answer sheet, if you are using one.

- Remember to go back to the difficult questions at the end of the test; sometimes, clues are given throughout the test that will provide you with answers.

- Note any negative words like *no* or *not*, and be sure your answer fits the question.

- Before changing an answer, be sure you have a very good reason to do so.

- Do not look for patterns on your answer sheet, if you are using one.

Copyright Protected

HELPFUL STRATEGIES FOR ANSWERING WRITTEN-RESPONSE QUESTIONS

A written response requires you to respond to a question or directive indicated by words such as explain, predict, list, describe, show your work, solve, or calculate. The following strategies can help you when answering written-response questions:

- Read and reread the question carefully.

- Recognize and pay close attention to directing words such as *explain*, *show your work*, and *describe*.

- Underline key words and phrases that indicate what is required in your answer, such as *explain*, *estimate*, *answer*, *calculate*, or *show your work*.

- Write down rough, point-form notes regarding the information you want to include in your answer.

- Think about what you want to say, and organize information and ideas in a coherent and concise manner within the time limit you have for the question.

- Be sure to answer every part of the question that is asked.

- Include as much information as you can when you are asked to explain your thinking.

- Include a picture or diagram if it will help to explain your thinking.

- Try to put your final answer to a problem in a complete sentence to be sure it is reasonable.

- Reread your response to ensure you have answered the question.

- Ask yourself if your answer makes sense.

- Ask yourself if your answer sounds right.

- Use appropriate subject vocabulary and terms in your response.

Not for Reproduction

TEST PREPARATION COUNTDOWN

If you develop a plan for studying and test preparation, you will perform well on tests.

Here is a general plan to follow seven days before you write a test.

COUNTDOWN: 7 DAYS BEFORE THE TEST

1. Use "Finding Out about the Test" to help you make your own personal test preparation plan.

2. Review the following information:

   – Areas to be included on the test

   – Types of test items

   – General and specific test tips

3. Start preparing for the test at least seven days before the test. Develop your test preparation plan, and set time aside to prepare and study.

COUNTDOWN: 6, 5, 4, 3, 2 DAYS BEFORE THE TEST

1. Review old homework assignments, quizzes, and tests.

2. Rework problems on quizzes and tests to make sure you still know how to solve them.

3. Correct any errors made on quizzes and tests.

4. Review key concepts, processes, formulas, and vocabulary.

5. Create practice test questions for yourself, and answer them. Work out many sample problems.

COUNTDOWN: THE NIGHT BEFORE THE TEST

1. Use the night before the test for final preparation, which includes reviewing and gathering materials needed for the test before going to bed.

2. Most importantly, get a good night's rest, and know you have done everything possible to do well on the test.

TEST DAY

1. Eat a healthy and nutritious breakfast.

2. Ensure you have all the necessary materials.

3. Think positive thoughts, such as "I can do this," "I am ready," and "I know I can do well."

4. Arrive at your school early, so you are not rushing, which can cause you anxiety and stress.

Copyright Protected

SUMMARY OF HOW TO BE SUCCESSFUL DURING A TEST

You may find some of the following strategies useful for writing a test:

- Take two or three deep breaths to help you relax.

- Read the directions carefully, and underline, circle, or highlight any important words.

- Look over the entire test to understand what you will need to do.

- Budget your time.

- Begin with an easy question or a question you know you can answer correctly rather than follow the numerical question order of the test.

- If you cannot remember how to answer a question, try repeating the deep breathing and physical relaxation activities. Then, move on to visualization and positive self-talk to get yourself going.

- When answering questions with graphics (pictures, diagrams, tables, or graphs), look at the question carefully, and use the following steps:

    1. Read the title of the graphic and any key words.

    2. Read the test question carefully to figure out what information you need to find in the graphic.

    3. Go back to the graphic to find the information you need.

- Write down anything you remember about the subject on the reverse side of your test paper. This activity sometimes helps to remind you that you do know something and are capable of writing the test.

- Look over your test when you have finished, and double-check your answers to be sure you did not forget anything.

Copyright Protected

PRACTICE TESTS

Table of Correlations

Specific Outcome	Practice Test 1	Practice Test 2
By the end of this course, students will:		
2 *Listen, speak, read, write, view and represent to comprehend literature and other texts in oral, print, visual and multimedia forms, and respond personally, critically and creatively*		
2.1.1.b use features found within a text as information to describe the communication situation within which the text was created		8, 14
2.1.2.a use a variety of strategies to comprehend literature and other texts and develop strategies for close reading of literature in order to understand contextual elements	2, 4, 6, 20, 26, 60	3, 6, 24, 28, 37, 38, 41, 52, 54, 55, 62
2.1.2.b paraphrase a text's controlling idea, and identify supporting ideas and supporting details	1, 3, 5, 11, 13, 15, 18, 30, 36, 46, 48	22, 51, 59
2.1.2.c summarize the plot of a narrative, describe its setting and atmosphere, describe development of conflict, and identify theme	8, 43, 47, 55, 68, 69	3, 9, 36, 42, 57
2.1.2.d describe the personality traits, motivations, attitudes, values and relationships of characters developed/persons presented in literature and other texts; and identify how the use of archetypes adds to an appreciation of text	16, 19, 28, 30, 32, 53, 56, 64, 65	4, 12, 13, 18, 25, 35, 50
2.1.2.e describe a text creator's tone, and relate tone to purpose and audience	13, 61,	
2.1.2.f differentiate between literal and figurative statements and between imagery and nonsensory language, identify symbols, recognize familiar allusions, and describe how images are developed in texts	6, 10, 22, 29, 42, 54	8, 14, 67
2.1.2.g describe visual elements and aural elements and describe their contributions to the meaning of texts	66	39, 56, 59
2.1.3.a reflect on and describe strategies used to engage prior knowledge as a means of assisting comprehension of new texts; and select, monitor and modify strategies as needed	21, 22	
2.1.3.c recall prior knowledge of rhetorical devices used in previously studied texts and textual elements and structures employed or developed to assist in understanding new texts	25, 26, 61	29, 33
2.1.3.d classify the genre/form of new texts according to attributes of genres/forms previously studied	12, 32	34
2.2.1.a identify a variety of text forms, including communications forms and literary forms and describe the relationships of form to purpose and content		40, 64
2.2.1.b describe audience factors that may have influenced a text creator's choice of form and medium		44
2.2.1.c describe a variety of organizational patterns and structural features that contribute to purpose and content	24, 62	40, 47, 48, 61
2.2.2.a describe rhetorical devices and stylistic techniques that create clarity, coherence and emphasis in print and nonprint texts	58, 63	52, 58, 62, 63
2.2.2.b describe aspects of a text that contribute to atmosphere, tone and voice	13, 25, 33, 40, 63	30, 46, 61, 63, 66
2.2.2.c recognize irony and satire in print and nonprint texts, and identify language used to create irony and satire	19, 57	5, 49, 60
2.2.2.d describe the effects of musical devices, figures of speech and sensory details in print and nonprint texts	10, 27, 31, 34, 38, 67	23, 31, 43, 46, 49, 61, 66

2.2.2.e recognize the use of motif and symbol in print and nonprint texts	39	16, 43
2.3.2.b assess the appropriateness of own and others' understandings and interpretations of works of literature and other texts, by referring to the works and texts for supporting or contradictory evidence	44, 47, 66	1, 19, 33, 36, 53
2.3.2.c describe settings and plots in terms of reality and plausibility, as appropriate	17, 33, 50, 51, 65	11, 15, 20, 26, 30, 32, 60
2.3.2.d describe character and characterization in terms of consistency of behaviour, motivation and plausibility	66	
2.3.2.e describe images in print and nonprint texts in terms of created reality and appropriateness to purpose	8, 18, 36, 45, 49, 52	17, 27, 48, 50, 63
2.3.3.a use terminology appropriate to the forms studied for discussing and appreciating the effectiveness and artistry of a variety of text forms	9, 12, 14, 37	29, 45, 47, 56, 64, 65
2.3.3.b describe the effectiveness of various texts, including media texts, for presenting feelings, ideas and information, and for evoking response	38, 40	59, 62
3 Listen, speak, read, write, view and represent to manage ideas and information		
3.2.1.a reflect on and describe strategies to determine the depth and breadth of inquiry or research and to identify the purpose, audience and potential forms of presentation	7	
3.2.1.c refine the purpose of inquiry or research by limiting or expanding the topic as appropriate	1, 23, 28, 35, 43, 46, 69	2, 7, 9, 11, 21, 33
4 Listen, speak, read, write, view and represent to create oral, print, visual and multimedia text, and enhance the clarity and artistry of communication		
4.1.1.c describe and address audience factors that affect text creation	9, 11	
4.1.2.d describe expectations and constraints of a communication situation, including assignment parameters, expected standards of quality and availability of resources; and select strategies to address expectations and constraints		10
4.2.4.b know and be able to apply capitalization and punctuation conventions correctly, including end punctuation, commas, semicolons, colons, apostrophes, quotation marks, hyphens, dashes, ellipses, parentheses, underlining and italics	59	
4.2.4.d identify and be able to use parts of speech correctly, including nouns, pronouns, verbs, adjectives, adverbs, prepositions, definite and indefinite articles, and coordinating and subordinating conjunctions	41	
4.2.4.g know and be able to use common sentence structures correctly—simple, compound, complex and compound-complex	41	

Copyright Protected

PRACTICE TEST 1

Read the following passage to answer questions 1 to 7.

THE NEW GLOBE THEATRE

The original Globe opened in 1599, burned down in 1613 but was immediately rebuilt that same year. After only 29 more years it was closed by the Puritans who felt theatre was a bad influence on society. They closed the Globe in 1642.

After almost 400 years, the Globe Theatre has been re-opened to the public again.
5 The reconstructed playhouse, built just 200 metres from the original site, was officially inaugurated by Her Majesty the Queen, on Thursday, June 12th, 1997. The opening season ran from May 29th to September 21st 1997. Since that first year, the new Globe has offered performances of plays by Shakespeare and his contemporaries on the type of stage for which they were written, many of them in original, 17th-century clothing.

10 After the Globe was closed by the Puritans in 1642, people lost track of its original design and layout. Only a few original documents remained and none of these provided an accurate picture of its design. Many people attempted to rebuild the Globe, either as only a drawing or as an actual building.

However, the successful attempt was begun in 1970 by one Mr. Sam Wanamaker,
15 who established the Shakespeare Globe Playhouse Trust. He found a suitable place of 0.4 hectare for the theatre on Bankside, but actual construction on the project only began in 1987. In 1982, former University of Alberta Professor John Orrell provided new evidence on the shape and dimensions of the Globe. His analysis of Wenceslas Hollar's "Long View of London" (1647)—a panorama of London drawn from the tower
20 of Southwark Cathedral—showed that the dimensions of the buildings depicted in the drawing were accurate. Thus, from Professor Orrell's analysis, researchers were able to determine that the measurements of the Globe depicted in the drawing were accurate as well.

The next breakthrough for the reconstruction project took place in 1989, when the
25 Globe's original foundations were discovered on Bankside, about two hundred yards from the reconstruction site. Although the Globe's original foundations are buried under the foundations of another building, archaeologists were able to discover the design of the original Globe using special underground sonar devices. This information was presented to the Globe's architects, who used it to give shape to the new theatre.

30 Not only did the builders remain faithful to the original design of the Globe, they also remained faithful to the traditional materials and techniques that were used on the original. Like the first Globe, the reconstructed theatre is built in a circle, with twenty wooden bays surrounding the stage, each three storeys high. These bays are constructed with reeds from Norfolk, and their walls are made with lime plaster. Similarly, the
35 stage is protected with a roof of interwoven reeds. Artisans carved the back wall in an elaborate, classical style. They built three doorways through which the audience enters and leaves the house. At the front, huge oak pillars on each side of the stage support the "heavens," the canopy painted with stars that hangs over the stage.

Although the Queen inaugurated the Globe in 1997, the theatre had been open to the
40 public since August 1994. Many visitors from around the world have come to visit the
Exhibition and see the Globe, both under construction and since it was finished. The
site was such a popular place to visit that on December 12th, 1996, Shakespeare's Globe
was voted the best attraction in Europe. It was awarded the European Tourism Initiative
Golden Star Award by the European Federation of Associations of Tourism Journalists.
45 The designers and builders of the Globe have opened a permanent exhibition. This
exhibition gives people an insight into the works of Shakespeare and the society in which
he lived and worked.

—Anonymous

1. Although the Queen inaugurated the new Globe Theatre on June 12th 1997, the new Globe had been opened to the public since

   A. 1970

   B. 1987

   C. 1994

   D. 1996

2. The new Globe theatre was constructed

   A. on the original site

   B. two hundred yards from the original site

   C. one hundred yards from the original site

   D. directly next to the original site

3. The reason why the new Globe is so famous **most likely** is that it

   A. showed that Shakespearean drama is timeless

   B. has received favourable reviews in the media

   C. has mounted many of Shakespeare's most popular plays

   D. faithfully reproduces so many aspects of the original Globe

4. Sam Wanamaker's contribution to the reconstruction of the Globe included

   A. drawing up plans for the building

   B. making sure many people heard about the project

   C. supervising the work on the building

   D. establishing a Trust Fund to help finance the project

5. Professor John Orrell presented evidence that shaped the design and layout of the new Globe. Which of the following statements **most accurately** describes this evidence?

   A. He discovered the colour and type of paint used on the original.

   B. He proved that the old site was only 200 yards from the new one.

   C. He proved that the dimensions of the old Globe in Hollar's drawing were accurate.

   D. He discovered a drawing by Wenceslas Hollar entitled, "Long View of London" (1647) that included the old Globe.

6. The canopy above the stage is called the "heavens" (line 38) because it

   A. is painted with stars

   B. is painted with images from theatrical history

   C. includes a portrait of Shakespeare himself

   D. includes a portrait of Sam Wanamaker, the founder of this project

7. The theatre is made up of _____ wooden bays.

   A. 15

   B. 20

   C. 25

   D. 30

Read the following passage to answer questions 8 to 14.

ON THE FUTURE OF POETRY

Poets of the Future! you that come
With striding march, and roll of drum,
What will your newest challenge be
To our prose-bound community?

5   What magic will you find to stir
The limp and languid listener?
Will it be daring and dramatic?
Will it be frankly democratic?

Will Pegasus[1] return again
10   In guise of modern aeroplane,
Descending from a cloudless blue
To drop on us a bomb or two?

I know not. Far be it from me
To darken dark futurity;
15   Still less to render more perplexed
The last vagary[2], or the next.

[1] Pegasus—a flying horse from ancient Greek mythology

[2] vagary—an unpredictable, or extravagant manifestation

I hold it for a certain thing,
That, blank or rhyming, song must sing;
And more, that what is good for verse,
20 Need not, by dint of rhyme, grow worse.

I hold that they who deal in rhyme
Must take the standpoint of the time—
But not to catch the public ear,
As mountebank[3] or pulpiteer;

25 That the old notes are still the new,
If the musician's touch be true—
Nor can the hand that knows its trade
Achieve the trite and ready-made;

That your first theme is Human Life,
30 Its hopes and fears, its love and strife—
A theme no custom can efface,
Common, but never commonplace;

—*by* Henry Austin Dobson

[3] mountebank—someone who boasts about things he has never done

8. In context, the phrase "prose-bound community" (line 4) could **most accurately** be defined as the people who
   A. love to read stories
   B. love television talk shows
   C. dislike reading in general
   D. dislike clubs and other organizations

9. From the context, "blank" verse (line 18) means verse that
   A. rhymes
   B. does not rhyme
   C. contains a distinct rhythm
   D. contains no distinct rhythm

10. The phrase "To drop on us a bomb or two" (line 12) is an example of
    A. simile
    B. metaphor
    C. hyperbole
    D. personification

11. The speaker of the poem addresses
    A. poets
    B. writers
    C. fellow readers
    D. literary historians

12. The verse structure of the poem contains an example of the
    A. sestet
    B. octave
    C. sonnet
    D. quatrain

13. Which of the following terms **most completely** summarizes the speaker's feelings about the future of poetry?
    A. terrified
    B. optimistic
    C. pessimistic
    D. ambivalent

14. Which of the following statements **best** summarizes the speaker's main theme of this poem?
    A. Poetry should rhyme.
    B. Poetry should be about human experience.
    C. Poetry should have a magic that stirs the reader.
    D. Poetry should be about unusual topics that excite the reader.

Read the following passage to answer questions 15 to 21.

STORIES OF GODS AND HEROES: THE WEDDING FEAST

Cepheus and his wife, with their future son-in-law Perseus and their daughter
Andromeda, repaired to the palace, where a wedding banquet was spread for them.
Everyone was filled with joy and feeling festive. Suddenly a noise was heard of warlike
clamor. Phineus, who had hoped to marry the bride himself, burst into the room with a

5 group of his friends, claiming Andromeda as his own. Cepheus protested, "You should
have made your bid for her earlier, before the marriage with Perseus was set." Phineus
made no reply, but hurled his javelin at Perseus. It missed its mark and fell harmlessly to
the floor. Perseus would have thrown his in turn, but the cowardly assailant ran and took
shelter behind the altar. His act was a signal for an onset by his band of friends upon

10 the wedding guests of Cepheus. They fought back in self-defense and a general conflict
began. The old king Cepheus retreated from the scene after fruitless shouts, calling the
gods to witness that he was not to blame for this outrageous violence erupting during the
wedding party.

Perseus and his friends were able to hold their own against Phineus's friends, but

15 the numbers of the assailants were too great for them and soon they began to tire.
Destruction seemed inevitable. A sudden thought struck Perseus, however: "I will make
my enemy the Gorgon, defend me." Then with a loud voice he exclaimed, "If I have any
friend here let him turn away his eyes!" and held up the head of the Gorgon. As you
know, anyone who looked directly at the terrible face of the Gorgon was turned to stone

20 immediately. "Seek not to frighten us with your tricks," said Phineus's friend Thescelus,
and raised his javelin to throw. He could not release the javelin because he was turned
to stone on the spot. Another friend, Ampyx, was about to plunge his sword into the
body of a Perseus's supporter, but his arm stiffened and he could neither thrust forward
nor withdraw it. Another, in the midst of a loud yell, stopped, his mouth open, but now

25 silent. Unfortunately, one of Perseus's friends, Aconteus, caught sight of the Gorgon and
stiffened like the rest. Phineus's friend Astyages struck him with his sword, but instead
of wounding Aconteus, it bounced off him with a ringing noise.

Phineus looked at this dreadful result of his unjust aggression from his hiding place and
felt confused. He called out to his friends, but got no answer. He touched them and

30 found they had all turned to stone. Turning his head away and falling on his knees he
stretched out his hands to Perseus and begged for mercy. "Take all," said he, "give me
but my life."

"Base coward," said Perseus, "thus much I will grant you; no weapon shall touch you;
moreover, you shall be preserved in my house as a memorial of these events." So saying,

35 he held the Gorgon's head to the side where Phineus was looking, and in the very
form in which he knelt, with his hands outstretched and face averted, he became fixed
immovably, a mass of stone!

---

15. What statement best describes the result of anyone looking directly at the face of the Gorgon?

   A. They turned to wood.

   B. They became furious.

   C. They froze like statues.

   D. They fell in love immediately.

16. Phineus invaded Perseus and Andromeda's wedding party because he

   A. was lonely

   B. was looking for a good time

   C. wanted to fight Perseus

   D. wanted to marry Andromeda himself

17. Phineus is described as a _____ for having thrown his javelin and run.

   A. hero

   B. fraid

   C. victim

   D. coward

18. The **main** moral of the myth of Perseus and Phineus is do not

   A. act in a cowardly manner

   B. interrupt your friend's wedding party

   C. look at enemies that can hurt you

   D. try to steal someone else's bride with violence

19. Why does Cepheus pray to the gods in the middle of the fight between Perseus' and Phineus' friends?

   A. He wanted them to stop fighting.

   B. He hoped for them to take him away.

   C. He wanted them to make sure Andromeda did not get hurt.

   D. He wanted them not to punish him for something that was not his responsibility.

20. How many of Phineus's followers died from looking at the Gorgon's head?

   A. 1

   B. 2

   C. 3

   D. 4

21. From the context of the story, we can assume that a javelin is **most like** a

   A. stone

   B. spear

   C. sharp sword

   D. strong hammer

Not for Reproduction

Read the following passage to answer questions 22 to 28.

THE GAME OF BILLIARDS

As they have been fighting two days, and have passed the night with their knapsacks on, beneath a flood of rain, the soldiers are completely exhausted. And yet for three mortal hours they have been left waiting, with grounded arms, in the puddles of the highroads and the mud of the saturated fields.

5   Benumbed by fatigue, by sleepless nights, and with their uniforms drenched with rain, they crowd together to warm and comfort one another. There are some who sleep standing, leaning against a neighbour's knapsack, and weariness and privations can be read distinctly upon those relaxed faces, overcome with sleep. Rain, mud, no fire, nothing to eat, a low, black sky, and the enemy in the air about. It is funereal.

10 What are they doing there? What is going on? The guns, with their muzzles pointed towards the wood, have the appearance of watching something. The soldiers stare fixedly at the horizon. Everything seems ready for an attack. Why do they not attack? What are they waiting for?

They are awaiting orders, and headquarters sends none. And yet the headquarters are not
15 far away. They are at yonder stately Louis-Treize château, whose red bricks, scoured by the rain, glisten among the trees half-way up the hill. Truly a princely dwelling, quite worthy to bear the banner of a marshal of France. Behind a broad moat and a stone wall which separate them from the road, smooth green lawns, lined with vases of flowers, extend to the porch. On the other side, the private side of the house, the hornbeam
20 hedges show luminous gaps; the pond in which swans are swimming lies like a mirror. Beneath the pagoda-like roof of an enormous aviary, peacocks and golden pheasants flash their wings and display their plumage, uttering shrill cries amid the foliage. Although the owners have gone away, one does not feel the abandonment, the desolation of war. The leader of the army has safeguarded even the tiniest flowers in the lawns, and it is
25 an impressive thing to find so near the battlefield that opulent tranquillity that is born of perfect order, of the accurate alignment of the shrubbery, of the silent depths of the avenues.

The rain, which fills the roads yonder with such disgusting mud, and digs such deep ruts, here is nothing more than an elegant, aristocratic shower, reviving the red of the
30 bricks and the green of the lawns, polishing the leaves of the orange-trees and the white feathers of the swans. Everything glistens, everything is peaceful. Really, but for the flag floating on the roof, but for the two soldiers on sentry-go before the gate, one would never suspect that it is the headquarters of an army. The horses are resting in the stables. Here and there one sees a groom, or an orderly in undress uniform, loitering about the
35 kitchen, or a gardener in red trousers placidly drawing his rake over the gravel in the great courtyards.

The dining-room, the windows of which look upon the porch, discloses a half-cleared table; uncorked bottles, soiled and empty glasses on the rumpled cloth; the end of a banquet, after the guests have gone. In the adjoining room one may hear loud voices,
40 laughter, the clicking of balls and the clinking of glasses. The marshal is playing his game of billiards, and that is why the army is waiting for orders. When the marshal had begun his game, the heavens might fall, but nothing in the world could prevent him from finishing it.

Billiards! that is the weakness of that great warrior. He stands there, as grave as in
45 battle, in full uniform, his breast covered with medals, with kindled eyes, flushed cheeks,
excited by feasting, grog, and the game. His aides-de-camp surround him, zealous and
respectful, uttering admiring exclamations at each of his strokes. When the marshal
makes a point, they all hasten to mark it; when the marshal is thirsty, they all rush to
prepare his grog. There is a constant rustling of the crisp uniforms, a jingling of medals.
50 To see all those sweet smiles, those artful, courtierlike reverences, all those new uniforms
and embroidery in that lofty apartment, with its oaken wainscoting, looking upon parks
and courts of honour, recalls the autumn days at Compiègne. This sight affords the eyes
a little rest from the stained cloaks that shiver yonder along the roads, forming such
sombre groups in the rain.

55 The marshal's opponent is a young captain of the staff, belted and curled and light-
gloved, who is in the first rank of billiard-players and capable of beating all the marshals
on earth. But he has the tact to keep a respectful distance behind his chief, and devotes
his energies to the task of not winning, and at the same time not losing too easily. He is
what is called an officer with a future.

60 Attention, young man, let us be on our guard! The marshal has fifteen, and you ten. The
point is to keep the game in that condition to the end. Then you will have done more for
your promotion than if you were outside with the others, beneath those torrents of water
which drown the horizon, soiling your natty uniform, tarnishing the gold of your medals
awaiting orders which do not come.

65 It is really an interesting game. The balls roll and clash and mingle their colours. The
cushions send them merrily back; the cloth waxes hot. Suddenly the flash of a cannon-
shot passes across the sky. A dull sound rattles the windows. Everybody starts, and they
look at each other anxiously. The marshal alone has neither seen nor heard anything;
leaning over the table, he is busily engaged in planning a magnificent draw-shot; draw-
70 shots are his strong point.

But there comes another flash, then another. The cannon-shots succeed each other in hot
haste. The aides-de-camp run to the windows. Can it be that the Prussians are attacking.

"Very well, let them attack!" says the marshal, chalking his cue. "It's your turn, captain."

The staff quivers with admiration. Turenne asleep upon a gun-carriage was nothing
75 compared to this marshal, who plays billiards so tranquilly at the moment of going into
action. Meanwhile the uproar redoubles. With the roar of the cannon is mingled the
rattle of musketry. A red steam, black at the edges, rises around the lawns. The whole
park is on fire. The terrified peacocks and pheasants shriek in the aviary; the Arabian
horses, smelling the powder, rear in the stables. The headquarters begins to be excited.

80 Despatch after despatch. Couriers arrive at full speed.

They ask for the marshal.

The marshal cannot be seen. Did I not tell you that nothing could prevent him from
finishing his game?

"It is your turn, captain."

Copyright Protected

85　But the captain is distraught. That is what it is to be young. Behold he loses his head, forgets his tactics, and makes two runs in succession, which almost give him the game. Thereupon the marshal becomes furious. Surprise and indignation animate his manly face. Just at this moment a horse ridden at a hard gallop rushes into the courtyard. A courier covered with mud forces his way past the sentries and ascends the steps at one

90　bound. "Marshal, marshal!" You should see how he is greeted. Puffing with anger and red as a rooster, the marshal appears at the window, his billiard-cue in his hand:

"What's the matter? What's all this? Isn't there any sentry there?"

"But, marshal—"

"All right, in a moment; wait for my orders, in God's name!"

95　And the window is violently closed. Wait for his orders! That is just what they are doing, the poor fellows. The wind drives the rain and the bullets full in their faces. Whole battalions are wiped out, while others stand useless, with their arms in readiness, utterly unable to understand their inaction. Nothing to do. They are awaiting orders. However, as one needs no orders to die, the men fall by hundreds behind the shrubs, in

100　the moats, in front of the great silent château. Even after they have fallen, the bullets tear them still, and from the open wounds the generous blood of France flows noiselessly. Above, in the billiard-room, it is getting terribly warm too; the marshal has recovered his lead, but the little captain is defending himself like a lion.

Seventeen! eighteen! nineteen!

105　They hardly have time to mark the points. The roar of the battle draws nearer. The marshal has but one more to go. Already shells are falling in the park. Suddenly one bursts over the pond. The mirror is shattered; a swan in deadly alarm swims wildly about amid an eddy of bloody feathers. That is the last stroke.

Then, a profound silence. Only the rain falling on the hedges, a confused rumbling at

110　the foot of the hill, and, along the muddy roads, a sound like the trampling of a hurrying flock. The army is in full retreat. The marshal has won his game.

—*by* Alphonse Daudet

22. The soldiers have been fighting for _____ days before this billiard game.

　A. 2

　B. 3

　C. 4

　D. 5

23. The "aviary" (line 21) could be **best** defined as the

　A. cellar where the meat was kept

　B. cages where the birds were kept

　C. barn where the horses were kept

　D. garage where the artillery was kept

24. The captain is an "officer with a future" (line 59) because he

   A. can lead his troops in battle

   B. can stand in the rain for long periods at a time

   C. knows not to upset his superior by beating him at billiards

   D. is very brave to play billiards while the cannons are whizzing by overhead

25. From the context of the narrative, who speaks the lines "Attention, young man, let us be on our guard! The marshal has fifteen, and you ten" (line 60)?

   A. The narrator

   B. The captain, to himself

   C. The leader of the army

   D. The officers who are watching the game

26. The general tells the soldiers to wait for his orders **mainly** because he knows that if he

   A. loses the billiard game, his soldiers will win the battle

   B. loses the billiard game, he will be angry at the captain

   C. wins the billiard game, his soldiers will win the battle

   D. wins the billiard game, he will throw a wonderful party

27. The reason so many soldiers are dying can **best** be explained by the

   A. marshall's love of billiards

   B. superior strength of the enemy

   C. rain has weakened the soldiers' resolve

   D. fact the captain does not dare beat the marshall

28. The billiard game serves as a metaphor for the

   A. battle

   B. winners

   C. dying soldiers

   D. bad weather outside

Copyright Protected

Not for Reproduction

Read the following passage to answer questions 29 to 35.

A CRITICAL RESPONSE TO ALPHONSE DAUDET'S A GAME OF BILLIARDS

Daudet works in a sort of fever. Even before beginning to write his books, he has related, acted, and almost "lived" them. This habit responds to a necessity of his nature, and this he also constitutes his process of composition. The original sketch is only an improvisation, but with the second version begins what he calls the painful part of
5 his labor.

He first abandons himself to his fancy, giving free rein to his troubadour instincts. The subject urges him on and outstrips him; his hand glides rapidly over the paper without writing all the words, or even pausing to punctuate, in the effort to follow the fever of his toiling brain by hastily stenographing ideas and sentiments.

10 Only with that "trembling of the fingers," with him a sign of inspiration, does he take up his pen. He at once launches into the full current of the action. As his figures are already "on foot in his mind," he loses no time in introducing them in full activity. The greater part of his novels consists in a series of pictures or episodes which pass in file beneath our eyes. There are no preludes either at the outset or in passing from one chapter to
15 another; he explains the situation by a word, leaving the reader to imagine such events as are not adapted to an entirely actual *mise en scène*. He renders only what moves his heart and sets his nerves in vibration—what is dramatic, picturesque, and animated in human affairs.

—*from* "The Literary Movement in France in the Nineteenth Century" (1893).

—*by* George Pellissier

---

29. The "painful part of his labour" (lines 4–5) when Daudet writes would **best** be described as
    A. writing the second draft
    B. improvising the first draft
    C. remembering where to put the punctuation
    D. reading the work that was just written

30. From the context, Daudet's "troubadour instincts" (line 6) could be described as his
    A. love of singing
    B. story-telling instincts
    C. pleasure over a well-sung melody
    D. enjoyment at hearing a good story

31. According to Pellissier, Daudet writes one of the drafts of his stories without punctuation because he

    A. writes too fast

    B. is a lazy writer

    C. does not want to waste ink on punctuation

    D. has not been taught to write properly

32. By stating that Daudet works in a sort of fever, Pellissier **probably** means that he

    A. is delirious when he writes

    B. works when he feels emotionally intense

    C. works best when he is not feeling very well

    D. uses characters that are almost always ill in some way

33. Pellissier states that a sign of inspiration for Daudet is

    A. quivering lips

    B. shaking knees

    C. sweating palms

    D. trembling fingers

34. The phrase "on foot in his mind" (line 12) serves as a metaphor to describe the

    A. excitement that he feels as his story jumps to life

    B. effort that is needed to bring his characters to life

    C. early movement of the characters in his imagination

    D. control that he needs to exercise over his imagination

35. According to Pellissier, what "sets [Daudet's] nerves in vibration" (line 17) could best be summarized as

    A. war stories

    B. human love affairs

    C. dramatic nature stories

    D. conflict and resolution between humans

Read the following passage to answer questions 36 to 42.

WHEN TO HER LUTE CORRINA SINGS

When to her lute[1] Corrina sings,
Her voice revives the leaden strings,
And does in highest notes appear,
As any challenged echo clear;
5 But when she does of mourning speak,
Even with her sighs the strings do break.

And as her lute does live or die,
Led by her passion, so must I,
For when of pleasure she does sing,
10 My thoughts enjoy a sudden spring,
But if she does of sorrow speak,
Even from my heart the strings do break.

—*by* Thomas Campion

---

[1] lute—from the 13th century; a stringed instrument having a large pear-shaped body, a vaulted back, a fretted fingerboard, and a head with tuning pegs which is often angled backward from the neck.

---

36. The phrase "her voice revives the leaden strings" (line 2) literally refers to how

A. beautifully Corrina plays the lute

B. beautiful the lute looks once it is revived

C. the lute strings are on the verge of dying

D. the strings echo Corrina's voice when she sings

37. According to the speaker, when Corrina sings, she sings about pleasure, but when she speaks, she speaks about

A. lutes

B. music

C. sorrow

D. challenges

38. The conjunction "But" appears in the second last lines of both verses (lines 5 and 11). The function of this conjunction would be best described as showing the

A. differences in the actions

B. comparison of unlike objects

C. contrasts between objects that are before and after

D. similarities between objects that are before and after

39. The shift from the first stanza to the second could be **most completely** described as a shift from

   A. Corrina's description of her singing to her speaking

   B. a second person to a first person point of view

   C. the speaker's description of Corrina to his own heart

   D. the speaker's description of Corrina's heart to her lute strings

40. The speaker's description of Corrina's lute living or dying by her passion (lines 7–8) **best** exemplifies which of the following poetic techniques?

   A. simile

   B. hyperbole

   C. onomatopoeia

   D. personification

41. When the speaker states that his thoughts "enjoy a sudden spring" (line 10) he **most likely** means

   A. his mind comes to life

   B. his mind always changes

   C. he feels as if he is drinking from a spring

   D. he feels as if his mind is bouncing like a spring

42. The rhyming patterns of the poem indicate it is comprised of

   A. free verse

   B. blank verse

   C. three quatrains for a total of twelve lines

   D. rhyming couplets

Read the following passage to answer questions 43 to 49.

A SUMMARY OF OEDIPUS THE KING

An oracle[1] told Laius, King of Thebes, that the child born to him by his queen Jocasta would kill his father and wed his mother. So when a son was born to them the infant's feet were riveted together and he was left to die on Mount Cithaeron.

5   But a shepherd found the babe and took care of him, and delivered him to another shepherd who took him to his master, the King of Corinth. Polybus being childless adopted the boy, who grew up believing that he was indeed the King's son.

Afterwards doubting his parentage he inquired of the Delphic god and heard himself the prophesy that had been declared before to Laius. The oracle told him, as well, that he was destined to kill his father and marry his mother. After hearing this he fled from
10   what he thought was his father Polybus's house. On his journey he encountered and unwittingly killed his father Laius at a crossroads.

---

[1] oracle—a person (as a priestess of ancient Greece) through whom a deity is believed to speak

Arriving at Thebes he answered the riddle of the Sphinx and the grateful Thebans made him their king. He reigned in the place of Laius, his father whom he had killed earlier. As the prophet had promised, he then married his real mother, the widowed queen
15 Jocosta. Children were born to them and Thebes prospered under his rule, but soon a terrible plague fell upon the city. Again the oracle was consulted and it told them to purge themselves of blood-guiltiness.

Oedipus denounces the crime of which he is unaware, and undertakes to track out the criminal. Step by step it is brought home to him that he himself is guilty of the crime
20 that makes the gods angry. In the end, Jocosta, his mother, commits suicide and Oedipus blinds himself and prays for death or exile.

—based on a play by Sophocles

43. Laius and Jocosta knew of their son's actions before he committed them because

   A. Oedipus consulted an oracle

   B. an oracle told the king of Thebes

   C. the king of Corinth could see into the future

   D. the priest of the oracle told Polybus

44. Oedipus was abandoned on

   A. Mount Thebes

   B. Mount Delphos

   C. Mount Acropolis

   D. Mount Cithaeron

45. According to this myth, Oedipus accidentally kills his father

   A. at a crossroads

   B. on the road to Corinth

   C. after trying to make peace with him

   D. after solving the riddle of the Sphinx

46. Oedipus becomes king because he

   A. was a savvy politician

   B. solved the riddle of the Sphinx

   C. knew how to achieve political success

   D. took his father's place in the kingdom

47. Although Oedipus did not know he had killed his father and married his mother, the gods still decided he was

A. guilty, and deserved to die

B. innocent of all wrong-doing

C. accountable for a minor infraction

D. guilty, and cursed with having to remain alive

48. The conclusion of the story can **best** be described as

A. inconclusive

B. a comic ending

C. creating a denouement

D. providing a form of justice

49. The statement that **best** summarizes the main theme of this myth is

A. "Always obey your parents"

B. "Shepherds are very kind people"

C. "It is wrong to marry your mother"

D. "It is impossible to escape one's fate"

Read the following passage to answer questions 50 to 56.

---

from ROMEO AND JULIET

ACT I. Scene I.

Verona. A public place.

[*Enter* **SAMPSON** *and* **GREGORY** *(with swords and bucklers) of the house of Capulet.*]

5   **SAMPSON**: Gregory, on my word, we'll not carry coals.

GREGORY: No, for then we should be colliers.

SAMPSON: I mean, and we be in choler[1], we'll draw[2].

GREGORY: Ay, while you live, draw your neck out of collar.

SAMPSON: I strike quickly, being moved.

10 **GREGORY**: But thou art not quickly moved to strike.

SAMPSON: A dog of the house of Montague moves me.

GREGORY: To move is to stir, and to be valiant is to stand. Therefore, if thou art moved, thou runn'st away.

SAMPSON: A dog of that house shall move me to stand. I will take the wall of any man

15 or maid of Montague's.

---

[1] choler—anger

[2] to draw—to draw swords and begin to fight

GREGORY: That shows thee a weak slave; for the weakest goes to the wall.

SAMPSON: 'Tis true; and therefore women, being the weaker vessels, are ever thrust to the wall. Therefore I will push Montague's men from the wall and thrust his maids to the wall.

20 **GREGORY**: The quarrel is between our masters and us their men.

SAMPSON: 'Tis all one. I will show myself a tyrant. When I have fought with the men, I will be cruel with the maids—I will cut off their heads.

GREGORY: The heads of the maids?

SAMPSON: Ay, the heads of the maids, or their maidenheads. Take it in what sense
25 thou wilt.

GREGORY: They must take it in sense that feel it.

SAMPSON: Me they shall feel while I am able to stand; and 'tis known I am a pretty piece of flesh.

GREGORY: 'Tis well thou art not fish; if thou hadst, thou hadst been poor-John. Draw
30 thy tool! Here comes two of the house of Montagues.

[*Enter two other Servingmen,* **ABRAM** *and* **BALTHASAR**]

SAMPSON: My naked weapon is out. Quarrel! I will back thee.

GREGORY: How? turn thy back and run?

SAMPSON: Fear me not.

35 **GREGORY**: No, marry. I fear thee!

SAMPSON: Let us take the law of our sides; let them begin.

GREGORY: I will frown as I pass by, and let them take it as they list.

SAMPSON: Nay, as they dare. I will bite my thumb at them[3]; which is disgrace to them, if they bear it.

40 **ABRAM**: Do you bite your thumb at us, sir?

SAMPSON: I do bite my thumb, sir.

ABRAM: Do you bite your thumb at us, sir?

SAMPSON: [*aside to* **GREGORY**] Is the law of our side if I say ay?

GREGORY: [*aside to* **SAMPSON**] No.

45 **SAMPSON**: No, sir, I do not bite my thumb at you, sir; but I bite my thumb, sir.

GREGORY: Do you quarrel, sir?

ABRAM: Quarrel, sir? No, sir.

SAMPSON: But if you do, sir, I am for you. I serve as good a man as you.

---

[3] to bite one's thumb—an offensive gesture, like swearing at a stranger

ABRAM: No better.

50 **SAMPSON**: Well, sir.

[*Enter* **BENVOLIO**]

GREGORY: [*aside to* **SAMPSON**]: Say 'better.' Here comes one of my master's kinsmen.

SAMPSON: Yes, better, sir.

55 **ABRAM**: You lie.

SAMPSON: Draw, if you be men. Gregory, remember thy swashing blow.

[*They fight*]

BENVOLIO: Part, fools! [*Beats down their swords*.] Put up your swords. You know not what you do.

60 [*Enter* **TYBALT**]

TYBALT: What, art thou drawn among these heartless hinds? Turn thee Benvolio, look upon thy death.

BENVOLIO: I do but keep the peace. Put up thy sword,
Or manage it to part these men with me.

65 **TYBALT**: What, drawn, and talk of peace? I hate the word
As I hate hell, all Montagues, and thee.
Have at thee, coward!

[*They fight*]

[*Enter an officer, and three or four* **CITIZENS** *with clubs or partisans*]

70 **OFFICER**: Clubs, bills, and partisans! Strike! beat them down!

CITIZENS: Down with the Capulets! Down with the Montagues!

[*Enter Old* **CAPULET** *in his gown, and his* **WIFE**.]

CAPULET: What noise is this? Give me my long sword, ho!

WIFE: A crutch, a crutch! Why call you for a sword?

75 **CAPULET**: My sword, I say!—Old Montague is come
And flourishes his blade in spite of me.

[*Enter Old* **MONTAGUE** *and his* **WIFE**]

MONTAGUE: Thou villain Capulet! Hold me not, let me go.

MONTAGUE'S WIFE: Thou shalt not stir one foot to seek a foe.

80 [*Enter* **PRINCE ESCALUS**, *with his Train*]

PRINCE: Rebellious subjects, enemies to peace,
Profaners of this neighbour-stained steel—
Will they not hear? What, ho! you men, you beasts,

That quench the fire of your pernicious rage
85 With purple fountains issuing from your veins!
On pain of torture, from those bloody hands
Throw your mistempered weapons to the ground
And hear the sentence of your moved prince.
Three civil brawls, bred of an airy word
90 By thee, old Capulet, and Montague,
Have thrice disturb'd the quiet of our streets
And made Verona's ancient citizens
Cast by their grave beseeming ornaments
To wield old partisans, in hands as old,
95 Cank'red with peace, to part your cank'red hate.
If ever you disturb our streets again,
Your lives shall pay the forfeit of the peace.
For this time all the rest depart away.
You, Capulet, shall go along with me;
100 And, Montague, come you this afternoon,
To know our farther pleasure in this case,
To old Freetown, our common judgment place.
Once more, on pain of death, all men depart.

[*Exeunt all but* **MONTAGUE**, *his* **WIFE**, *and* **BENVOLIO**]

105 **MONTAGUE**: Who set this ancient quarrel new abroach?
Speak, nephew, were you by when it began?

BENVOLIO: Here were the servants of your adversary
And yours, close fighting ere I did approach.
I drew to part them. In the instant came
110 The fiery Tybalt, with his sword prepar'd;
Which, as he breath'd defiance to my ears,
He swung about his head and cut the winds,
Who, nothing hurt withal, hiss'd him in scorn.
While we were interchanging thrusts and blows,
115 Came more and more, and fought on part and part,
Till the Prince came, who parted either part.

MONTAGUE'S WIFE: O, where is Romeo? Saw you him to-day?
Right glad I am he was not at this fray.

BENVOLIO: Madam, an hour before the worshipp'd sun
120 Peer'd forth the golden window of the East,
A troubled mind drave me to walk abroad;
Where, underneath the grove of sycamore
That westward rooteth from the city's side,
So early walking did I see your son.

—*by* William Shakespeare

Copyright Protected

50. From the context we can infer that Gregory tells Sampson to say that his master is "better" (line 52) because he

    A. suddenly feels brave

    B. wants them to tell the truth

    C. wants Sampson to get into a fight with Abram

    D. notices that their master is coming and that they wouldn't have to fight for long

51. Sampson and Gregory are the _____ .

    A. servants of the house of Montague

    B. servants from the house of Capulet

    C. butlers from the house of Montague

    D. kitchen staff from the house of Capulet

52. The main purpose of the servants' conversation is to

    A. practise their jokes on each other

    B. convince each other of their bravery

    C. demonstrate how intelligent they are

    D. show that people from the Capulet's house are dangerous

53. When Benvolio and Tybalt meet it is obvious that

    A. Benvolio would like to make peace

    B. Benvolio is a coward

    C. Tybalt tells too many jokes

    D. Tybalt would like to make peace

54. When the prince states: "Your lives will pay the forfeit of the peace" (line 97) he probably means the Montagues and Capulets will

    A. be sent home the next time

    B. have to give up the idea of peace forever

    C. have to die the next time violence erupts

    D. be charged a fine the next time violence breaks out

55. From Lady Montague's statement, "Right glad I am [Romeo] was not at this fray," (line 118) we can infer Lady Montague

    A. wishes she knew her son better

    B. wants to speak with Romeo about his troubled mind

    C. fears for her son's safety if he had been involved in this fight

    D. fears Romeo might have killed Tybalt had he been in this fight

56. According to Benvolio, during this fight Romeo was

    A. talking with some friends about Juliet

    B. resting in the shade of some trees in the evening

    C. walking by the sea in the early morning sun light

    D. resting under some sycamore trees in the morning

Read the following passage to answer questions 57 to 63.

PART TWO: NATURE XII

To hear an oriole sing
May be a common thing,
Or only a divine.

It is not of the bird
5 Who sings the same, unheard,
As unto crowd.

The fashion of the ear
Attireth that it hear
In dun[1] or fair.

10 So whether it be rune[2],
Or whether it be none,
Is of within;

The "tune is in the tree,"
The skeptic showeth me;
15 "No, sir! In thee!"

—by Emily Dickinson

---

[1] dun—dull or drab

[2] rune—magic, mystery

---

57. In the poem, the phrase "only a divine" (line 3) is ironic because

    A. experiencing something divine is common and ordinary

    B. divinely inspired events take place around us every day

    C. divine is contrasted with the word "common"

    D. everybody has something divine in them

58. The **most likely** explanation for "crowd" (line 6) not rhyming with "bird" (line 4) and "unheard" (line 5) is that it

    A. emphasizes the busyness of crowds of people

    B. shows that crowds of people usually move too fast

    C. contrasts the sound of the crowds with the song of the oriole

    D. shows how most people in crowds do not hear the sounds of birds

59. From the context, the **best** definition of "Attireth" (line 8) is to

   A. dress

   B. undress

   C. become fatigued

   D. hear in a particular way

60. The function of the semi-colon at the end of the fourth stanza is **probably** to

   A. provide some variety in the rhythm of the poem

   B. show how carefully the author utilizes punctuation

   C. allow the reader a breath before continuing to the end of the poem

   D. show how the idea expressed in the fourth verse contrasts with that of the fifth

61. Which of the following phrases **best represents** the speaker's concluding line, "No sir! In thee" (line 15)?

   A. The skeptic thinks that trees sing.

   B. The skeptic cannot hear very well.

   C. The speaker thinks that how one listens determines whether the bird sounds magical.

   D. The speaker thinks that listening carefully will allow one to hear beautiful music even in crowds.

62. The **main** purpose of the short lines and verses in this poem is to

   A. make the poem easier to write

   B. keep the poem simple for easier reading

   C. keep the poem simple so the skeptic will better understand

   D. echo the trills of the oriole that the speaker is describing

63. This poem does not contain any images or symbols, **most likely** because the

   A. speaker is focused on telling a story

   B. speaker realizes that crowds are often quite noisy

   C. poem emphasizes the importance of hearing clearly

   D. symbols would weaken the impact of the beautiful oriole

Read the following passage to answer questions 64 to 70.

ELEONORA

Hand in hand about this valley, for fifteen years, roamed I with Eleonora before love entered within our hearts. It was one evening at the close of the third lustrum of her life, and of the fourth of my own, that we sat locked in each other's embrace, beneath the serpent-like trees, and looked down within the waters of the River of Silence at our
5   images therein. We spoke no words during the rest of that sweet day, and our words even upon the morrow were tremulous and few. We had drawn the god Eros from that wave, and now we felt that he had enkindled within us the fiery souls of our forefathers. The passions which had for centuries distinguished our race came thronging with the fancies for which they had been equally noted, and together breathed a delirious bliss
10   over the Valley of the Many-Coloured Grass. A change fell upon all things. Strange, brilliant flowers, star-shaped, burst out upon the trees where no flowers had been known before. The tints of the green carpet deepened, and when, one by one, the white daisies shrank away, there sprang up in place of them, ten by ten of the ruby-red asphodel. And life arose in our paths, for the tall flamingo, hitherto unseen, with all gay glowing birds,
15   flaunted his scarlet plumage before us. The golden and silver fish haunted the river, out of the bosom of which issued, little by little, a murmur that swelled at length into a lulling melody more divine than that of the harp of Æolus, sweeter than all save the voice of Eleonora. And now, too, a voluminous cloud, which we had long watched in the regions of Hesper, floated out thence, all gorgeous in crimson and gold, and settling in peace
20   above us, sank day by day lower and lower until its edges rested upon the tops of the mountains, turning all their dimness into magnificence, and shutting us up as if for ever within a magic prison-house of grandeur and of glory.

The loveliness of Eleonora was that of the angels; but she was a maiden artless and innocent as the brief life she had led among the flowers. No guile disguised the fervour
25   of love which animated her heart, and she examined with me its inmost recesses as we walked together in the Valley of the Many-Coloured Grass, and discoursed of the mighty changes which had lately taken place therein.

At length, having spoken one day, in tears, of the last sad change which must befall humanity, she thenceforward dwelt only upon this one sorrowful theme, interweaving it
30   into all our converse, as, in the songs of the bard of Schiraz, the same images are found occurring again and again in every impressive variation of phrase.

She had seen that the finger of Death was upon her bosom—she had been made perfect in loveliness only to die; but the terrors of the grave to her lay solely in a consideration which she revealed to me one evening at twilight by the banks of the River of Silence.
35   She grieved to think that, after her coming death I would bury her in the Valley of the Many-Coloured Grass, I would quit for ever its happy recesses, transferring the love which now was so passionately her own to some maiden of the outer and every-day world.

And then and there I threw myself hurriedly at the feet of Eleonora, and offered up a vow
40   to herself and to Heaven, that I would never bind myself in marriage to any daughter of Earth—that I would in no manner prove recreant[1] to her dear memory, or to the memory of the devout affection with which she had blessed me. And I called the Mighty Ruler of the Universe to witness the pious solemnity of my vow. And the curse which I invoked of Him and of her, a saint in Elusion, should I prove traitorous to that promise, involved a

---

[1] recreant—unfaithful to duty or allegiance

Copyright Protected

45 penalty the exceeding great horror of which will not permit me to make record of it here.
And the bright eyes of Eleonora grew brighter at my words; and she sighed as if a deadly
burthen had been taken from her breast; and she trembled and very bitterly wept; but she
made acceptance of the vow (for what was she but a child?), and it made easy to her the
bed of her death. And she said to me, not many days afterwards, tranquilly dying, that,
50 because of what I had done for the comfort of her spirit, she would watch over me in that
spirit when departed, and, if so it were permitted her, return to me visibly in the watches
of the night; but, if this thing were indeed beyond the power of the souls in Paradise, that
she would at least give me frequent indications of her presence; sighing upon me in the
evening winds, or filling the air which I breathed with perfume from the censers of the
55 angels. And, with these words upon her lips, she yielded up her innocent life, putting an
end to the first epoch of my own.

But let me on.—Years dragged themselves along heavily, and still I dwelled within the
Valley of the Many-Coloured Grass; but a second change had come upon all things. The
star-shaped flowers shrank into the stems of the trees, and appeared no more. The tints
60 of the green carpet faded; and, one by one, the ruby-red asphodels withered away; and
there sprang up, in place of them, ten by ten, dark, eye-like violets, that writhed uneasily
and were ever encumbered with dew. And Life departed from our paths; for the tall
flamingo flaunted no longer his scarlet plumage before us, but flew sadly from the vale
into the hills, with all the gay glowing birds that had arrived in his company. And the
65 golden and silver fish swam down through the gorge at the lower end of our domain, and
bedecked the sweet river never again. And the lulling melody that had been softer than
the wind-harp of Æolus, and more divine than all save the voice of Eleonora, it died little
by little away, in murmurs growing lower and lower, until the stream returned, at length,
utterly into the solemnity of its original silence; and then, lastly, the voluminous cloud
70 uprose, and, abandoning the tops of the mountains to the dimness of old, fell back into
the regions of Hesper, and took away all its manifold golden and gorgeous glories from
the Valley of the Many-Coloured Grass.

Yet the promises of Eleonora were not forgotten; for I heard the sounds of the swinging
of the censers of the angels; and streams of a holy perfume floated ever and ever about
75 the valley; and at lone hours, when my heart beat heavily, the winds that bathed my brow
came unto me laden with soft sighs; and indistinct murmurs filled often the night air; and
once—oh, but once only! I was awakened from a slumber, like the slumber of death, by
the pressing of spiritual lips upon my own.

But the void within my heart refused, even thus, to be filled. I longed for the love which
80 had before filled it to overflowing. At length the valley pained me through its memories
of Eleonora, and I left it for ever for the vanities and the turbulent triumphs of the world.

I found myself within a strange city, where all things might have served to blot from
recollection the sweet dreams I had dreamed so long in the Valley of the Many-Coloured
Grass. The pomps and pageantries of a stately court, and the mad clangour of arms, and
85 the radiant loveliness of woman, bewildered and intoxicated my brain. But as yet my
soul had proved true to its vows, and the indications of the presence of Eleonora were
still given me in the silent hours of the night. Suddenly, these manifestations ceased; and
the world grew dark before mine eyes; and I stood aghast at the burning thoughts which
possessed—at the terrible temptations which beset me. For there came from some far, far
90 distant and unknown land, into the court of the king I served, a maiden to whose footstool

I bowed down without a struggle in the most ardent, in the most abject worship of love. What indeed was my passion for the young girl of the valley in comparison with the fervour and the delirium, and the spirit-lifting ecstasy of adoration with which I poured out my whole soul in tears at the feet of the ethereal Ermengarde?—Oh, bright was the
95 angel Ermengarde! and in that knowledge I had room for none other.—Oh, divine was the angel Ermengarde! and as I looked down into the depths of her memorial eyes, I thought only of them—and of her.

I wedded;—nor dreaded the curse I had invoked; and its bitterness was not visited upon me. And once—but once again in the silence of the night, there came through my lattice
100 the soft sighs which had forsaken me; and they modelled themselves into familiar and sweet voice, saying—

"Sleep in peace!—for the Spirit of Love reigneth and ruleth, and, in taking to thy passionate heart her who is Ermengarde, thou art absolved, for reason which shall be made known to thee in Heaven, of thy vows unto Eleonora."

—*by* Edgar Allen Poe

64. After the narrator and Eleonora spend time together in the Valley of the Many-Coloured Grass, the
  A. vegetation began to take on more vibrant colours
  B. plant life began to wither and die
  C. the sun held its place in the sky
  D. the animals gathered around to watch them

65. According to the narrator, Eleonora becomes upset because she
  A. knows she is about to die
  B. fears that he will forget about her
  C. knows she will be leaving him behind after she dies
  D. does not want to be buried in the Valley of the Many-Coloured Grass

66. The phrase that **best** summarizes the narrator's initial feelings for Eleonora is he
  A. loved her deeply
  B. was sorry he ever met her
  C. felt a deep antipathy towards her
  D. did not care much one way or the other

67. After Eleonora dies, the narrator leaves the country for the
  A. city
  B. valley
  C. afterlife
  D. mountains

68. The narrator's curse does not fall on him, even though he has broken his promise to Eleonora, because
    A. Eleonora had given him her blessing
    B. its time limit had run out
    C. he was not under its effect in the city
    D. the narrator had been faithful to Eleonora by loving Ermengarde

69. The statement that **best** summarizes the theme of this story is
    A. love conquers all, no matter the situation
    B. loving someone who is alive is more important than someone who has died
    C. if you love someone with all your heart, nature will take on more vibrant colours
    D. it is okay to break promises to someone, as long as you love the next person you are with

Copyright Protected

ANSWERS AND SOLUTIONS—PRACTICE TEST 1

1. C	11. A	21. B	31. A	41. A	51. B	61. C
2. B	12. D	22. A	32. B	42. D	52. B	62. D
3. D	13. B	23. B	33. D	43. B	53. A	63. C
4. D	14. B	24. C	34. C	44. D	54. C	64. A
5. C	15. C	25. A	35. D	45. A	55. C	65. B
6. A	16. D	26. C	36. D	46. B	56. C	66. A
7. B	17. D	27. D	37. C	47. D	57. A	67. A
8. A	18. D	28. A	38. C	48. D	58. D	68. A
9. B	19. D	29. A	39. C	49. D	59. D	69. B
10. C	20. C	30. B	40. D	50. D	60. D	

1. C

According to paragraph seven, the Queen "inaugurated the Globe in 1997," but the theatre had been open since August 1994. The other dates refer to different stages in the re-construction process. In 1970, Sam Wanamaker began the project by setting up a trust fund. On December 12th, 1996, the Globe was voted the best attraction in Europe. Since the opening sentence states that the new Globe has re-opened nearly 400 years after it was closed, is not as specific an answer as August, 1994.

2. B

The fifth paragraph states that the new Globe has been built nearly 200 yards from the original site of the Globe. Since none of the other answers are correctly reflected in the passage they can be discarded.

3. D

Although each of the other answers also contribute to the fame of the new Globe theatre, each of these is derived from the response, that "it faithfully reproduces so many aspects of the original Globe". If the re-construction had not successfully reproduced so many features of the original, it would not have received as many favourable reviews in the media. Since many theatres mount Shakespearean plays this fact by itself could not account for the new Globe's popularity.

4. D

From the responses that are offered here, **D** most clearly represents Mr. Wanamaker's contribution to the construction of the new Globe. Although the passage states that he also found a suitable site for the building, none of the other responses include this information and therefore can be safely disregarded.

5. C

According to the passage, former University of Alberta English professor, Dr John Orrell demonstrated that the dimensions of the buildings in Hollars's drawing of the area were accurate. From this information the architects were then able to extrapolate the dimensions of the old Globe theatre that was among the buildings in Hollars's drawing. Although, Orrell researched Hollars's drawing, the information presented is not as relevant to the question. Therefore it, and the others are not successful responses.

6. A

While the other responses are perhaps plausible to some degree, the second last paragraph in this text provides the evidence that satisfies this question. This paragraph states that the canopy is painted with stars.

7. B

Like question 6, question 7 requires you to accurately provide the facts that satisfy the question. Once the fact has been discovered in the passage, you can save time by discarding the rest of the responses. The passage states that there were twenty wooden bays in the theatre.

8. A

Although we might think that these days, fewer people enjoy reading prose than do watching television or movies, the speaker is comparing these prose-readers with the even smaller number of people who read poetry. The prose-bound community thus would exclude the people who dislike reading in general, the people who enjoy clubs and other community organizations, and the people who love television talk shows.

9. B

Even though we may not be certain about the meaning of "blank verse", we can assume that it refers to verse that does not rhyme because in the context of the poem it is placed in opposition to verse that does rhyme (line 18). Since blank verse is placed in this position, verse that rhymes could be ruled out. For the same reason, verse with a distinct rhythm, and verse that is confusing could be ruled out as well.

10. C

The phrase "To drop on us a bomb or two" is an example of hyperbole, a poetic technique that uses exaggeration for rhetorical effect. Both simile and metaphor refer to comparisons between unlike objects.

11. A

It might seem reasonable to assume that the speaker of a poem about the future of poetry could be addressing either fellow readers, literary historians, or fellow writers of poetry. The very first phrase that opens the poem states: "Poets of the future!"

12. D

As you know from your studies in English literature, the quatrain is a verse structure with four lines. The sestet has six; the octave eight; and the sonnet fourteen. Each of the verses in "On the Future of Poetry" consist of four lines.

13. B

Although the speaker states that he does not know about the future of poetry (line 13), which would appear to indicate that "ambivalent" is the strongest response, the speaker continues on to offer advice to future poets. The fact that he supposes that poets may indeed benefit from his suggestions indicates that he feels optimistic to some degree about the future of poetry. None of the other responses reflect this positive tone and therefore can be safely disregarded.

14. B

According to lines 29 and 30, the speaker says that "… your first theme is Human Life,/ Its hopes and fears, its love and strife." Although the speaker suggests that good poetry should "sing" (line 18), he also states that that singing should derive not from 'magic' nor striking topics, but from human experience. Although the poem itself does rhyme, the speaker states that poetry either with or without rhyme can be effective, thus ruling out this response as a successful answer.

15. C

Since none of the choices offered here state that the offenders who looked directly at the Gorgon turned to stone, the best answer, the one that comes closest to this sense, "froze like statues." "They turned to wood," is not accurate enough. Both "they became furious" and "they fell in love immediately" are not supported by evidence from the text, and therefore are not correct responses.

Copyright Protected

16. D

The strongest answer is the one that most specifically describes Phineus's motives for invading the wedding party. Although he does want to prevent Andromeda from marrying Perseus, this statement does not express his reasons for wanting to block their marriage. The other statements could be plausible motives, but since they are not explicitly stated by the text they can be dismissed from your consideration.

17. D

Phineus is described as a coward for throwing his javelin and running. Once you have discovered this factual information from the text, you do not need to absorb more time by considering the accuracy of the other responses.

18. D

The strongest response in this case is the one that most completely reflects the meaning of the events in the story. Although Phineus does interrupt his friend's wedding party, he does much more than that as well. The precept to not act in a cowardly manner may well be true, but in the application with this Greek myth, Phineus does more than act like a coward. Before he runs he has violently broken into a room full of people and nearly killed one of them. Therefore the strongest response of the number offered here, would have to be "do not try to steal someone else's bride with violence."

19. D

You must infer from the text the correct answer for this question, since the text does not offer any directly. Since he pleads with them to notice that he has done no wrong in the wedding fight that has broken out, you can infer that his first concern in relation to the gods is that they do not take an action against him as a result of this fight. Although the other answers here might be worthy responses for a pacifist, an escapist, or a father, none of these responses qualify because they do not correspond with the evidence that is provided by the text.

20. C

According to the text, three of Phineus's supporters were turned to stone as a result of looking at the Gorgon's head. One of Perseus's friends also died. And later Phineus himself was frozen on the spot by the head. The question specifically asks us for the number of Phineus's friends that are killed.

21. B

From the context we could ascertain that the javelin is most like a spear, even if we had never seen a javelin before. The verb, "to raise" implies that the javelin was lifted for the purposes of throwing. This verb thus eliminates hammer and sword. The act of raising also places stone in doubt as a suitable response, since the verb implies that a relatively heavy object is being lifted in preparation for a throw. The strongest answer is spear.

22. A

The opening paragraph states that the soldiers have been fighting for two days before the billiard game begins. Once you have found that information you can safely disregard the other answers.

23. B

Even if you did not know that an aviary was a large confined place where birds were kept, so they could fly around but not go free, you could nonetheless discover the answer from the other information that the text provides. Since it is peacocks and pheasants shrieking in the aviary, none of the other responses could satisfy this question.

24. C

The narrator states that the office has a future because "he has the tact to keep a respectful distance behind his chief, and devotes his energies to the task of not winning, and at the same time not losing too easily." He may be able to stand in the rain for long periods at a time, but since he does not have to in this narrative, this response is not relevant to our considerations. Likewise, he may be brave to play with cannons whizzing by, but he continues in the presence of this officer to restrain himself from winning.

25. A

Although it may seem strange for the narrator to turn from us, his audience of readers, to address one the characters in his story, this technique has the effect of making the story's action seem as though it continues independent of us reading about it or the narrator describing it. None of the other responses that are offered make sense in this context and therefore must be dismissed.

26. C

The best answer, of all the ones offered here, indicates that the general believes that if he wins the billiard game his soldiers will win the battle. Based on the information provided by the story this is the best possible answer you could infer. You may guess what might have happened had the general lost and the officer won (they're both from the same army, so wouldn't the soldiers outside still win against the advancing army?) But since the story does not let you know what might have happened, you can only base your answer on what actually does.

27. D

According to the narrator, the war ends when the billiard game ends. From this fact you can infer that the battle continues because the billiard game continues. Had the captain beaten the marshal in short order, the battle would have been finished as well. The marshal does love to play billiards, but expects to win. It seems that this fact prevents the soldiers from being saved, as the captain avoids winning to end the game. In the end, you recognize the connection the story is attempting to make between the battlefield and the billiard table.

28. A

The story at first seems confusing, as the military leaders insist on finishing a billiard game while the opposing army advances and begins shelling their billiard room. Once the game is completed, and with it the battle, the metaphor of battle serving to explain the conflict of billiards becomes apparent.

29. A

At the end of the first paragraph Pellissier states that writing the second draft causes Daudet the most hardship. As with the other factual answers, once you have discovered the answer that satisfies the question, you may move on without wasting time considering the merits of the other responses.

30. B

Since you know that troubadours were a class of lyric poets who flourished from the 11th to the end of the 13th century, you can infer that Daudet's troubadour instincts are those that helps him tell a good story. The other answers that refer to singing are not as relevant to those involving his story-telling practices.

31. A

Each writer has a different writing style. The lack of punctuation in one of Daudet's drafts does not indicate that he is lazy, ignorant, or frugal. Instead it further demonstrates the emotional intensity with which Daudet writes, and with that, the speed at which the words come out of his pen onto the page.

32. B

By stating that Daudet works in a sort of fever Pellissier refers to the emotional intensity that grips Pellissier as he writes. Perhaps this intensity is reflected in his narrator's turn to exhort one of the characters in the story, as if they were really living and breathing independent of his creation.
This emotional intensity does not point to some illness on Daudet's part and therefore allows you to strike those responses off the list of possibilities.

33. D

The information is provided for us in the third paragraph: "Only with that 'trembling of the fingers,' with him a sign of inspiration…" The other answers describe a physiological response that might be possible in the act of writing, but since they do not describe as specifically the particular response that Daudet experiences, they could not be correct answers.

Copyright Protected

34. C

According to Pellissier, the characters already begin stirring in Daudet's imagination before he begins to write, and he is obliged to catch up to them as he gets his writing underway. Although Daudet does feel some excitement as his story begins, the movement of the characters in his imagination, is a sign of his characters beginning to take on a life of their own.

35. D

What apparently animates Daudet is "what is dramatic, picturesque, and animated in human affairs." Although the other responses, love affairs, nature stories, and war stories, could potentially make fascinating narratives, the only response that reflects the particular information offered about Daudet is **D**, and thus this is the only correct answer.

36. D

This figure of speech is known as personification. Thus, the lute itself does not literally become revived from the singing. Instead its strings support, or "echo," her voice as she accompanies herself.

37. C

When Corrina speaks, it is of "sorrow" (line 11). Although you would not be wrong to state unhappiness, the fact that sorrow is actually named in the poetic text makes the most specific and thus the most successful response. She does make music on her lute, but neither of these answers addresses the terms that are raised by the question, and therefore could not be correct.

38. C

The strongest answer of those offered here, reflects the usual function of the conjunction "but." The function that this word performs is called "disjunctive." A disjunctive word signals a break between statements that both precede and follow.

39. C

How can you tell from this poem that a shift takes place from the first to the second stanzas? Although the second stanza opens with a reference to the lute, as did the first stanza, the line that follows offers the clue. The first person singular pronoun "I" at the end of the line indicates that the speaker has shifted his thoughts from their focus on Corrina to a new focus on the effect that Corrina has on himself (lines 8 and 10). A shift from a second to a first person narrator, would be indicated by a shift in pronouns, from the second person singular "you" to the first person singular "I." Although the "I" is used in the second stanza its presence is implied in the first, by the fact that the same speaker is speaking throughout the poem.

40. D

The fact that an inanimate object like the lute is given human characteristics such as living and dying, means this technique is called personification.

A simile is an indirect comparison using *like* or *as*. Hyperbole refers to the use of exaggeration to create a rhetorical effect. Onomatopoeia occurs when a word imitates a sound. None of these responses relates to the terms of the question and therefore could not be successful.

41. A

The most satisfactory answer is the one that addresses most fully the condition of the speaker's mind in the presence of his beloved Corrina. To say that his thoughts 'spring up', misses the implications of the metaphor. Since a mind does not literally "spring up" to anywhere, we would have to infer that this figure of speech refers to the quickening, or awakening of the speaker's mind.

42. D

When two lines that follow each other rhyme we call them rhyming couplets. Free verse follows neither a rhythmic metre nor a rhyming pattern. Blank verse could have a rhythmic metre but no rhyme scheme. Neither of these terms apply here so they can be dismissed. Although the total number of lines in this poem is twelve, they are not organized in four line quatrains, thus ruling out this answer as well.

43. B

This answer requires a careful reading of the text in order to keep the facts of the narrative straight. Since Oedipus is the one of whom the oracle speaks, "Oedipus consulted an oracle", would not be correct. According to the evidence of the first line from this text, the king is told by an oracle about Oedipus's future, thus rendering **B** the most valid response.

44. D

The last sentence in the first paragraph states that Oedipus was abandoned on Mount Cithaeron so that he would have no chance of fulfilling the oracle's prophecy. Ironically, it's because he is placed on this mountain that the chain of events begin which lead to the prophecy's fulfillment. None of the other mountains are identified with Oedipus in this context, and therefore the responses can be disregarded.

45. A

The third paragraph states that Oedipus killed his father at a crossroads, not knowing that it was his father that he was fighting against. The story indicates that Oedipus arrives at Thebes, after killing his father.

46. B

The narrative states that the final step Oedipus took that placed him in the throne once held by his father, and by extension, in the position of husband to his mother, was that of solving the riddle of the Sphinx. The narrative does not indicate that Oedipus had political aspirations. The last distractor merely restates the question and could not therefore be a correct answer.

47. D

The law of the gods in Greek myths is the same as the law of Western societies: ignorance of the law does not excuse one from the rule of law. Although you might not think it fair that Oedipus should be punished for unwittingly committing a crime, according to the information presented in the myth, Oedipus is declared guilty of committing a crime, and is forced to live.

48. D

The ending is neither comic nor inconclusive. And since you know that a dénouement is an up-turn in the ending of a tragedy that indicates the possibility of hope, **C** could not be a satisfactory response either.

49. D

The fact that Oedipus's fate continues to evolve no matter what steps are taken to avoid it, indicates that, "it is impossible to escape one's fate," is the most successful answer. Although the other statements each represent a truth of some kind, none of them could be considered a theme of this passage excerpted from the myth of Oedipus.

50. D

Immediately after telling Sampson to give the answer that will goad their opponents into drawing their swords, Gregory states: "Here comes one of my master's kinsmen." This statement indicates that Gregory realizes they would not really have to fight anyway, allowing them to talk more bravely than they should. "He suddenly feels brave" is close to being a correct response. This bravery is derived not from his willingness to fight.

51. B

The opening instructions to the play identify the servants as working in the house of Capulet.

52. B

Although their jokes indicate that they have some intelligence, the main theme of each of them shows that they are trying to out-brag each other about their own feelings of bravery. From their exchange, you do not get a sense of how dangerous the Capulet's household has become.

53. A

When Benvolio and Tybalt meet it is obvious that Benvolio would like to make peace. He says to Tybalt: "I do but keep the peace. Put up thy sword, Or manage it to part these men with me." In Romeo and Juliet Tybalt is a rash character who neither tells jokes nor tries to make peace. Benvolio has drawn his sword in order to convince the others to put theirs away. From this action we can tell that he is not a coward.

54. C

From the context of the passage you can infer that the prince means that if peace is broken, the fine will be paid with the lives of those who broke this peace. "They will be charged a fine the next time violence breaks out" does not represent this situation strongly enough. "Peace will have to be given up forever," represents the situation too strongly. "Everyone will be sent home the next time" is not stated in the text, and so should be discarded as well.

55. C

Lady Montague's statement indicates that she would have feared for Romeo's safety had he been at this fight. Since you can infer that Romeo's melancholy feelings have caused him to walk by the sea at dawn, you can also infer that Romeo would not have been in the same edgy mood that characterizes Tybalt.

56. C

Benvolio tells Lady Montague that Romeo was "walking by the sea in the early morning sun light." This first image of Romeo avoiding the company of friends, unable to sleep comfortably indicates that something is troubling him. This first love that makes him feel melancholy is soon forgotten when he sees Juliet for the first time.

57. A

Although it may be that "everybody has something divine in them", or that "divinely inspired events take place around us every day", the irony in this line as it is offered in this particular poem, indicates that the irony derives from the description of the divine as common and ordinary.

58. D

The poetic technique of rhyme appeals to the reader's ear. The jarring sound of "crowds" after the rhyming sounds of "bird" and "heard," emphasizes not the monotonous hum the crowds make, but the deafness of crowds to beautiful sounds around them like the songs of a bird.

59. D

The verb "Attireth" is used metaphorically to represent the different ways the ear can hear a particular sound. The first two distracters do not express this metaphorical level of meaning, and thus would have to be discarded. "To become fatigued," does not address even the literal meaning expressed in the poem, rendering this a failing response.

60. D

A semi-colon indicates a disjunction between the phrases that precede and follow the punctuation. The fourth verse states that the effect of a sound comes from within the listener; the fifth verse begins with a sceptic saying "the tune is in the tree." The semi-colon does show how carefully Dickinson uses punctuation in this poem, but since this answer and the others, do not refer to the way this punctuation contributes to the poem's effect, they are not satisfactory responses.

61. C

The sceptic believes that sounds are most importantly external to the listener, since that is from where they originate. The speaker on the other hand believes that the most important aspect of hearing lies not with the source of the sound (such as the bird's song) but with the internal experience of the listener.

62. D

Writers of poetry try to remain aware not only of the content they are writing about in the poem, but also the way the form of the poem affects that content. In this example, Dickinson's poem about the song of a bird is echoed in the poem's structure. In the lines of the poem the reader can also hear the song of the bird. Although a shorter poem may seem easier to read, this apparent ease can be deceptive if you fail to realize the role that the form is playing in relation to the meaning.

63. C

You can assume that the poet would have been able to think of some symbols, if she had intended to use them. The relation between the noise of crowds and the lack of images is not clear. Likewise, the relation between symbols and a weakened impact of the oriole in the poem is not clear either.

64. A

The narrator states that the vegetation began to take on more vibrant hues once he and Eleonora began spending time in the Valley. Whether the vegetation actually did become more brightly coloured, or whether this greater intensity was only something they perceived, being in love, is not important for the story. Although other myths have described the Sun holding its position in the sky, or the animals gathering to watch a beautiful scene unfold, these elements are not included in this narrative, and thus cannot be included in your answer.

65. B

In the fourth paragraph the narrator states that Eleonora's concern is that he will "transfer the love which now was so passionately her own to some maiden of the outer … world." "She fears that he will forget about her," expresses Eleonora's fear. None of the other selections actually cause Eleonora to grieve. Her knowledge of her death, as well as her burial in the Valley of the Many-Coloured Grass are events about which she feels at peace.

66. A

The narrator explains in the first paragraph how he fell in love with Eleonora. The term "antipathy" refers to a strong feeling against another person. Even if you have never seen this word before, you can still discover its meaning by considering the words from which it is built: "anti," as you know, means "against"; "pathy" refers to emotions, or feelings. A common word with this stem is "sympathy", meaning "to feel the same feelings as another person." By carefully using inference, you can find the correct responses, even of terms that you have never studied before.

67. A

In the second last paragraph the narrator states that he "found himself in a strange city." The other choices do not merit your attention once you have discovered this evidence in the text.

68. A

The narrative concludes with the voice of Eleanor speaking from the dead: "Sleep in peace!—for the Spirit of Love reigneth and ruleth, and, in taking to thy passionate heart her who is Ermengarde, thou art absolved, for reason which shall be made known to thee in Heaven, of thy vows unto Eleonora."

69. B

Eleanora's blessing from the grave over the narrator's new relationship implies that "loving someone who is alive is more important than someone who has died". The other statements may express truths of one kind or another, but only this first statement most completely summarizes the information that is presented in the story.

Copyright Protected

PRACTICE TEST 2

Read the following passage to answer questions 1 to 7.

EMMA

Emma Woodhouse, handsome, clever, and rich, with a comfortable home and happy disposition, seemed to unite some of the best blessings of existence; and had lived nearly twenty-one years in the world with very little to distress or vex her.

She was the youngest of the two daughters of a most affectionate, indulgent father; and
5 had, in consequence of her sister's marriage, been mistress of his house from a very early period. Her mother had died too long ago for her to have more than an indistinct remembrance of her caresses; and her place had been supplied by an excellent woman as governess, who had fallen little short of a mother in affection.

Sixteen years had Miss Taylor been in Mr. Woodhouse's family, less as a governess than
10 a friend, very fond of both daughters, but particularly of Emma. Between them it was more the intimacy of sisters. Even before Miss Taylor had ceased to hold the nominal office of governess, the mildness of her temper had hardly allowed her to impose any restraint; and the shadow of authority being now long passed away, they had been living together as friend and friend very mutually attached, and Emma doing just what she
15 liked; highly esteeming Miss Taylor's judgment, but directed chiefly by her own.

The real evils, indeed, of Emma's situation were the power of having rather too much her own way, and a disposition to think a little too well of herself; these were the disadvantages which threatened alloy to her many enjoyments. The danger, however, was at present so unperceived, that they did not by any means rank as misfortunes
20 with her.

Sorrow came—a gentle sorrow—but not at all in the shape of any disagreeable consciousness.—Miss Taylor married. It was Miss Taylor's loss which first brought grief. It was on the wedding-day of this beloved friend that Emma first sat in mournful thought of any continuance. The wedding over, and the bride-people gone, her father and
25 herself were left to dine together, with no prospect of a third to cheer a long evening. Her father composed himself to sleep after dinner, as usual, and she had then only to sit and think of what she had lost.

The event had every promise of happiness for her friend. Mr. Weston was a man of unexceptionable character, easy fortune, suitable age, and pleasant manners; and there
30 was some satisfaction in considering with what self-denying, generous friendship she had always wished and promoted the match; but it was a black morning's work for her. The want of Miss Taylor would be felt every hour of every day. She recalled her past kindness—the kindness, the affection of sixteen years—how she had taught and how she had played with her from five years old—how she had devoted all her powers to attach
35 and amuse her in health—and how nursed her through the various illnesses of childhood. A large debt of gratitude was owing here; but the intercourse of the last seven years, the equal footing and perfect unreserve which had soon followed Isabella's marriage, on their being left to each other, was yet a dearer, tenderer recollection. She had been a friend and companion such as few possessed: intelligent, well-informed, useful, gentle,
40 knowing all the ways of the family, interested in all its concerns, and peculiarly interested in herself, in every pleasure, every scheme of hers—one to whom she could speak every thought as it arose, and who had such an affection for her as could never find fault.

How was she to bear the change?—It was true that her friend was going only half a mile from them; but Emma was aware that great must be the difference between a
45 Mrs. Weston, only half a mile from them, and a Miss Taylor in the house; and with all her advantages, natural and domestic, she was now in great danger of suffering from intellectual solitude. She dearly loved her father, but he was no companion for her. He could not meet her in conversation, rational or playful.

The evil of the actual disparity in their ages (and Mr. Woodhouse had not married early)
50 was much increased by his constitution and habits; for having been a valetudinarian[1] all his life, without activity of mind or body, he was a much older man in ways than in years; and though everywhere beloved for the friendliness of his heart and his amiable temper, his talents could not have recommended him at any time.

—by Jane Austen

[1] valetudinarian—a person of a weak or sickly constitution; especially one whose chief concern is being or becoming a chronic invalid

1. Although Emma's mother dies when she is young, she is raised by a

   A. manservant

   B. sister

   C. governess

   D. family friend

2. From the context of the passage, the word "nominal" (line 11) **most probably** means

   A. to nominate

   B. in name only

   C. Miss Taylor was not a very good governess

   D. Miss Taylor was a very good governess

3. According to this passage, the **main** reason Emma's situation is fraught with evils is because she

   A. lives in the country-side

   B. has no brothers to protect her

   C. has gotten used to getting her own way

   D. lost her mother at an early age

4. The change that Emma finds nearly unbearable is

   A. she now has to go to work

   B. she cannot visit her friend

   C. the governess has gotten married

   D. her father has decided to remarry

5. Miss Taylor marries Mr. Weston when Emma is

  A. 5 years of age

  B. 11 years of age

  C. 16 years of age

  D. 21 years of age

6. The phrase that **best** describes Mr. Weston's character is he was

  A. irritable and high-strung

  B. relaxed and basically lazy

  C. easy-going and well-to-do

  D. physically fit and polite

7. The **best** explanation of why Emma's father is not good company for her is he was

  A. the lord of an estate

  B. not as witty as she was

  C. much older than she was

  D. occupied with more important things

Read the following passage to answer questions 8 to 13.

LOVE AND FASHION

[*The Drawing Room at* **LORD ARDVILLE***'s.*]

HILARIA: The secret must 'ere now be revealed to Miss Exbury. My heart is very heavy about this good and dear old lord; and not very light, I am afraid, about his son! How odd it is I never can get that Valentine out of my head! Do what I will, try how I
5 may, turn which way I can,—still he rises uppermost in my thoughts. If it had not been for Sir Archy—but how glad I am I resisted! Yet I have never been happy since!—but I have been happy—so nobody has found it out. [*Enter* **LORD EXBURY**.] My lord!

LORD EXBURY: [**VALENTINE***'s father*] I thought I should have met you in the room with my Daughter.

10 **HILARIA:** Shall I call Miss Exbury, my lord?

LORD EXBURY: By no means. I have stated to her all it is essential she should learn, and I am better satisfied to speak with you alone.

HILARIA: Should he name Valentine!—[*aside.*]

LORD EXBURY: The solemn trust with which my friend, your Father, left you to my
15 guardianship, your residence in my family, and still more, if possible, the endearing disposition with which you have captivated all our hearts—

HILARIA: He is coming to Valentine!—[*aside.*]

Copyright Protected

LORD EXBURY: —Are circumstances which do not give me more pleasure, from the confidence with which they urge me to treat you, than pain, at this moment, from the
20 nature of my present communication.

HILARIA: I am sure, my lord, if I thought—I am sure, my lord, I—I—He will plead for Valentine, and I shall never withstand him! [*aside.*]

LORD EXBURY: The evil which must now burst publicly upon my house, has long hung upon my apprehensions; yet, while I saw any chance it might be averted, I confined
25 them to my own bosom. The time is over now for concealment: it is over for hope! In one word, I must renounce the world for the present myself, or know I shall leave my children to obscurity and distress.

HILARIA: Is it possible!

LORD EXBURY: You will easily trace the cause to its source: the extravagances of
30 my son Mordaunt are at least not darkened by hypocrisy, for he does not more carelessly involve than unconcernedly betray himself—not, alas!—as you will know—from frankness of character, but from deeming it fine to be wholly indifferent to the opinions and the feelings of others.

HILARIA: I have long feared he was imprudent, but suspected not how widely.

35 **LORD EXBURY**: Three or four years of retirement and economy may yet retrieve his fortune and credit, and enable me to secure his sister's portion from any mischief through a future relapse into the same courses: for though I mean severely to probe, and hope a little to touch him, I dare not build upon much stability of repentance from a disposition which submits to be guided by the fluctuating breath of Fashion.

40 **HILARIA**: How I grieve for you, my lord!—yet—I wish he would not speak with such contempt of Fashion! [*aside.*]

LORD EXBURY: Numberless have been my efforts to convince his mind, and induce him to retrench his expences: but there is a madness in the times that sets Reason at naught, and commits conviction to punishment. His creditors are now come upon him
45 in a body, his resources are at an end, and his character, and my name—are disgraced together!

HILARIA: Your name? O no, my lord! Your name, established by your own unsullied life, must be respected as long as it can be remembered.

LORD EXBURY: Yesterday he confessed to me his situation, and informed me of
50 a compromise to which his creditors had agreed, but which he had no means to fulfil without my aid. As he seasoned the avowal by a promise to be wholly directed by me, I formed at once the plan I am now going to execute: I ordered the immediate discharge of all my servants, the sale of my town house and furniture—

HILARIA: Oh!

55 **LORD EXBURY**: And that both my villas should be let upon a three years lease. I then sent off Davis in search of a cheap asylum for myself and family.

HILARIA: I am thunderstruck!

LORD EXBURY: Yet I then thought I had three Weeks before me for preparation; but when I acquainted my Brother Ardville with my design, his reluctance to lose sight of
60 his fair Enslaver, precipitated the proposals of which the failure has caused this general breach. The violence of his displeasure, which obliges me thus suddenly to quit his house, forces from me also this abrupt communication. Your cousin, Sir Archy Fineer, who has been agent, I find, for Mordaunt, with his chief creditors, has come hither this morning to acquaint us that the compromise is arranged. All is now ready for our
65 removal. I grieve for my poor Girl; but Mordaunt engages to subscribe to any reform; and Valentine—

HILARIA: I wish I were safe in town! [*aside.*]

LORD EXBURY: Valentine, whose little independent fortune, left him by his aunt, is in no danger from this storm, has youth, and, I think, talents. I am not uneasy for him. He
70 will be my best support.

HILARIA: What next! [*aside.*]

LORD EXBURY: But with regard to you, my dear Hilaria—I have, indeed, much solicitude[1]: I cannot expect you should shut yourself up with us in the country—

HILARIA: Indeed, my lord, if you knew half my concern for this affair—or half the
75 reverence I bear for you—

LORD EXBURY: I know your kindness of Heart, & am but too sensible of the loss we shall all sustain by the deprivation of your society—though you will permit me, I trust, to hope we shall not entirely lose sight of you? Where-ever you fix your abode, you will come to us, I must flatter myself, sometimes, for a week or two, in the summer?

80 **HILARIA:** In the summer? My dearest Lord Exbury!—my honoured Guardian!—I will come to you at all seasons—or, rather, I will quit you in none! Take me with you, my dear lord, whither so ever you go!

LORD EXBURY: My amiable Ward! You oblige, penetrate me!—From Valentine—

HILARIA: I am undone! [*aside.*]

—*by* Frances Burney

[1] solicitude—attentive care and protectiveness; also an attitude of solicitous concern or attention

8. Miss Hilaria states that she cannot "get that Valentine out of [her] head" (line 4). From the context of the passage, she probably means she

A. cannot forget him

B. is in love with him

C. needs to protect him from disaster

D. knows he has gotten into her head

9. According to Lord Exbury, his family is forced to sell their estate and move to more humble quarters because his

   A. son Morduant has many debts

   B. wife has left him for another man

   C. son Valentine has spent all the family fortune

   D. actions have resulted in some poor business deals

10. Hilaria's statement, "I am undone," (line 84) **most likely** means she fears

    A. she will still have to live with Lord Exbury's family, even though she wishes she were free of them

    B. she will not be able to live with Lord Exbury's family anymore

    C. her secret love of Morduant will be discovered by Lord Exbury

    D. her attraction to Valentine will be discovered by Lord Exbury

11. The **main** purpose of Hilaria's asides is to

    A. show the audience her thoughts

    B. distance the audience from Hilaria

    C. help us sympathize with Lord Exbury

    D. represent the dangers involved with keeping secrets from a lover's parent

12. Select the phrase that **most completely** describes the action Lord Exbury has chosen to assist Morduant.

    A. Punish him by having him sent to jail

    B. Reward him by giving him half his estate

    C. Protect him by giving him quarters at his mansion

    D. Save him by selling his estate to pay off his creditors

13. From the passage, you can infer that Hilaria wishes to stay with Lord Exbury's family when they move because she

    A. has no family of her own

    B. has an attachment to Valentine

    C. feels attached to their family

    D. wishes to continue working for Lord Exbury

Read the following passage to answer questions 14 to 20

THE MYSTERIOUS MARRIAGE

[*The outer wall and gate-way of a magnificent Castle, with an ascent, and distant view of the entrance.* **OSMOND** *and* **UBERTO** *meeting.*]

OSMOND: YOU come from the chase, Uberto: what's the sport?

UBERTO: Sport! marry, such sport as had well nigh cost us our lives, and our friends
5 some score of masses.

OSMOND: You roused then the boar!

UBERTO: I warrant you we did, and to some purpose too! An I e'er rouse another
such, I'll give him leave to make a dinner of me. But for our brave guest, the Lord
Sigismond, I question whether our souls had not come to tell you whereabouts they had
10 left our bodies.—In my life shall I never forget how he churned and tore up the ground
with rage! And what's most strange, methought, when his eyes glared with the greatest
fury, he always looked full upon me. Yet I had not offended him either; for if some
people's valour did not lie nearer the point of their lance than mine, the boar might have
made his breakfast in the forest, and we ours in the castle, without either of us taking a
15 fancy to a limb of the other.

OSMOND: But, Sigismond!

UBERTO: True! he's a hero—and your hero, I suppose, has a life or two more to
spare than your commoner. Briefly, however, he advanced, brandished his spear with a
determined look—as—thus!—and—I will not wrong my honesty so far as to say I saw
20 him kill the monster—But this I will certify—I saw the monster dead, and heard our
whole troop shout to the honour of Sigismond.

OSMOND: 'Tis a brave youth!

UBERTO: And courteous too; I warrant he's nobly born!

OSMOND: At least he's nobly bred.

25 **UBERTO**: And methinks love could not devise a better match of gentleness, than
betwixt him and my lord's young favourite, the Lady Constantia.

OSMOND: Trust me, no!
Uberto, there's a secret spring of blood
That bids the obscure still soar! 'Tis Nature's touch;
30 Who thus would mock the avarice[1] of Fortune,
Wooing her from her own! He'll no Constantia!
Nay much I err too, or our beauteous Countess
Beholds the young and gallant Sigismond
With more than friendly gaze. Come, come, thou'st marked it.

35 **UBERTO**: Why truly I have seen some glances pass between them, that it were worth
more than my head to recount to my lord. For, despite of what nature may do in the heart
of his daughter, she will never, I trust, move his heart into thinking, that all these

---
[1] avarice—excessive or insatiable desire for wealth or gain

Copyright Protected

noble titles and princely domains should fall into the hands of a vagrant stranger—and a prisoner too.

40 **OSMOND**: He had ne'er been a prisoner but in the cause of the Count. Thou knowest that on the day my lord and his daughter were taken captive by a band of wandering Poles—this young stranger—this valiant Sigismond, stood forth to save her from dishonour, and drew his sabre even against his countrymen.

UBERTO: Yes; and his countrymen rewarded him for it by leaving him in our hands!—
45 What a tale dost thou tell me, as if I was not in at the rescue; and did not with my good sword—

OSMOND: Nay, good Uberto—keep but thy tongue as quiet as thy sword, and— [*music*]—Peace! the hunters!—'tis the horn of Sigismond.

—*by* Harriet Lee

14. The **best** explanation for Uberto's breathlessness when first meeting Osmond is he

   A. was nearly killed by a wild boar

   B. had run some distance from the hunting party

   C. was excited to speak with Uberto about Lord Sigismond

   D. had been thinking about Constantia just before meeting Osmond

15. Uberto and Osmond consider Sigismond to be a 'hero' because he

   A. spent some time in prison

   B. killed a boar with his spear

   C. performed his duties for the Count

   D. has fallen in love with the lovely Constantia

16. Although we do not meet Sigismond directly, the conversation about him indicates that he is

   A. brave

   B. gallant

   C. cowardly

   D. handsome

17. According to Osmond, Sigismond has been a prisoner because he was

   A. innocent and was unfairly punished

   B. merely performing his duties for the Count

   C. showing what he would do to win Constantia

   D. justly punished for a crime he committed

18. Even though Sigismond is a foreigner in the country of Osmond and Uberto, he was abandoned by his own countrymen because he

    A. betrayed them

    B. found their company boring

    C. had become a loyal friend of the Count

    D. defended Constantia from their attempted kidnapping

19. The **main** meaning of Osmond's speech to Uberto regarding Sigismond's attraction for Constantia is

    A. Constantia and Sigismund are made for each other

    B. Sigismond is not good enough for Constantia

    C. Constantia has not even noticed Sigismond

    D. Sigismond is trying to woo Constantia

20. The fact that this conversation about love between Sigismond and Constantia takes place in the context of boar hunting **most likely** implies that

    A. both are male hobbies

    B. the two actions are contrastingly different

    C. one involves killing; the other involves nurturing

    D. the two actions are considered similar

Read the following passage to answer questions 21 to 27.

EVE'S RANSOM

An hour later he was at Old Square, waiting for the tram to Aston. Huge steam-driven vehicles came and went, whirling about the open space with monitory bell-clang. Amid a press of homeward-going workfolk, Hilliard clambered to a place on the top and lit his pipe. He did not look the same man who had waited gloomily at Dudley Port; his eyes
5 gleamed with life; answering a remark addressed to him by a neighbour on the car, he spoke jovially.

No rain was falling, but the streets shone wet and muddy under lurid lamp-lights. Just above the house-tops appeared the full moon, a reddish disk, blurred athwart floating vapour. The car drove northward, speedily passing from the region of main streets and
10 great edifices into a squalid district of factories and workshops and crowded by-ways. At Aston Church the young man alighted, and walked rapidly for five minutes, till he reached a row of small modern houses. Socially they represented a step or two upwards in the gradation which, at Birmingham, begins with the numbered court and culminates in the mansions of Edgbaston.

15 He knocked at a door, and was answered by a girl, who nodded recognition.

"Mrs. Hilliard in? Just tell her I'm here."

There was a natural abruptness in his voice, but it had a kindly note, and a pleasant smile accompanied it. After a brief delay he received permission to go upstairs, where the door

---

of a sitting-room stood open. Within was a young woman, slight, pale, and pretty, who
20 showed something of embarrassment, though her face made him welcome.

"I expected you sooner."

"Business kept me back. Well, my niece?"

The table was spread for tea, and at one end of it, on a high chair, sat a child of four years
old. Hilliard kissed her, and stroked her curly hair, and talked with playful affection.
25 This little girl was his niece, the child of his elder brother, who had died three years ago.
The poorly furnished room and her own attire proved that Mrs. Hilliard had but narrow
resources in her widowhood. Nor did she appear a woman of much courage; tears had
thinned her cheeks, and her delicate hands had suffered noticeably from unwonted
household work.

30 Hilliard remarked something unusual in her behaviour this evening. She was restless,
and kept regarding him askance, as if in apprehension. A letter from her, in which she
merely said she wished to speak to him, had summoned him hither from Dudley. As a
rule, they saw each other but once a month.

"No bad news, I hope!" he remarked aside to her, as he took his place at the table.

35 "Oh, no. I'll tell you afterwards."

Very soon after the meal Mrs. Hilliard took the child away and put her to bed. During
her absence the visitor sat brooding, a peculiar half-smile on his face. She came back,
drew a chair up to the fire, but did not sit down.

"Well, what is it?" asked her brother-in-law, much as he might have spoken to the
40 little girl.

"I have something very serious to talk about, Maurice."

"Have you? All right; go ahead."

"I—I am so very much afraid I shall offend you."

The young man laughed.

45 "Not very likely. I can take a good deal from you."

She stood with her hands on the back of the chair, and as he looked at her, Hilliard saw
her pale cheeks grow warm.

"It'll seem very strange to you, Maurice."

"Nothing will seem strange after an adventure I've had this afternoon. You shall hear
50 about it presently."

"Tell me your story first."

"All right, I'll tell you. I met that scoundrel Dengate, and—he's paid me the money he
owed my father."

"He has paid it? Oh! really?"

55 "See, here's a cheque, and I think it likely I can turn it into cash. The blackguard has
been doing well at Liverpool. I'm not quite sure that I understand the reptile, but he

seems to have given me this because I abused him. I hurt his vanity, and he couldn't resist the temptation to astonish me. He thinks I shall go about proclaiming him a noble fellow. Four hundred and thirty-six pounds; there it is."

60 He tossed the piece of paper into the air with boyish glee, and only just caught it as it was fluttering into the fire.

"Oh, be careful!" cried Mrs. Hilliard.

"I told him he was a scoundrel, and he began by threatening to thrash me. I'm very glad he didn't try. It was in the train, and I know very well I should have strangled him. It
65 would have been awkward, you know."

"Oh, Maurice, how can you—?"

"Well, here's the money; and half of it is yours."

"Mine? Oh, no! After all you have given me. Besides, I sha'n't want it."

"How's that?"

70 Their eyes meet Hilliard again saw the flush in her cheeks, and began to guess its explanation. He looked puzzled, interested.

"Do I know him?" was his next inquiry.

"Should you think it very wrong of me?" She moved aside from the line of his gaze. "I couldn't imagine how you would take it."

75 "It all depends. Who is the man?"

Still shrinking towards a position where Hilliard could not easily observe her, the young widow told her story. She had consented to marry a man of whom her brother-in-law knew little but the name, one Ezra Marr; he was turned forty, a widower without children, and belonged to a class of employers of labour. The contrast between such a man and
80 Maurice Hilliard's brother was sufficiently pronounced; but the widow nervously did her best to show Ezra Marr in a favourable light.

"And then," she added after a pause, while Hilliard was reflecting, "I couldn't go on being a burden on you. How very few men would have done what you have—"

"Stop a minute. Is that the real reason? If so—"

85 Hurriedly she interposed.

"That was only one of the reasons—only one."

Hilliard knew very well that her marriage had not been entirely successful; it seemed to him very probable that with a husband of the artisan class, a vigorous and go-ahead fellow, she would be better mated than in the former instance. He felt sorry for his
90 niece, but there again sentiment doubtless conflicted with common-sense. A few more questions, and it became clear to him that he had no ground of resistance.

"Very well. Most likely you are doing a wise thing. And half this money is yours; you'll find it useful."

—by George Gissing

21. Hilliard was a different man after visiting Dudley Port because
   A. money owing was paid to his father
   B. he was paid money that had been owed to him
   C. Mrs. Hilliard had invited him over for dinner
   D. he was paid money that had been owed to his father

22. The literary technique of _____ is represented in Hilliard calling Dengate a "reptile" (line 56)
   A. simile
   B. metaphor
   C. hyperbole
   D. personification

23. Maurice says that he is glad Dengate did not try to thrash him in the train because he would have
   A. received a beating with everyone watching
   B. had nowhere to run
   C. been unable to get him
   D. strangled him with everyone watching

24. According to Mrs. Hilliard, she will not take half of Maurice's money despite his offer because
   A. she would rather have his affections
   B. he has done so much for her already
   C. she does not need the money
   D. he does really needs the money for other things

25. The reason that **best** explains Mrs. Hilliard's invitation to Maurice is she
   A. was eloping with Ezra Marr
   B. had just been paid 436 pounds
   C. was getting married to Ezra Marr
   D. had some strange news to tell Maurice

26. We can infer from the narrative that Mrs. Hilliard is reluctant to tell Maurice the news of her engagement because
   A. Ezra Marr comes from a lower social standing than Maurice
   B. Ezra Marr is an employer with a lot of money
   C. she has to describe him in the best light
   D. she fears Maurice's anger

27. The phrase "no ground of resistance" (line 91) **most likely** means

A. she was able to resist him

B. he could not resist her approach

C. he felt he was losing ground to her

D. she had no reason for refusing his offer of financial support

Read the following passage to answer questions 28 to 34.

ON BOARD THE TYPHOON

I do not remember much about the voyage to Boston, for after the first few hours at sea I was dreadfully unwell.

The name of our ship was the "A No. 1, fast-sailing packet Typhoon." I learned afterwards that she sailed fast only in the newspaper advertisements. My father owned
5   one quarter of the Typhoon, and that is why we happened to go in her. I tried to guess which quarter of the ship he owned, and finally concluded it must be the hind quarter— the cabin, in which we had the cosiest of state-rooms, with one round window in the roof, and two shelves or boxes nailed up against the wall to sleep in.

There was a good deal of confusion on deck while we were getting under way. The captain
10 shouted orders (to which nobody seemed to pay any attention) through a battered tin trumpet, and grew so red in the face that he reminded me of a scooped-out pumpkin with a lighted candle inside. He swore right and left at the sailors without the slightest regard for their feelings. They didn't mind it a bit, however, but went on singing—

"Heave ho!
15 With the rum below,
And hurrah for the Spanish Main O!"

I will not be positive about "the Spanish Main," but it was hurrah for something O. I considered them very jolly fellows, and so indeed they were. One weather-beaten tar in particular struck my fancy—a thick-set, jovial man, about fifty years of age, with
20 twinkling blue eyes and a fringe of gray hair circling his head like a crown. As he took off his tarpaulin I observed that the top of his head was quite smooth and flat, as if somebody had sat down on him when he was very young.

There was something noticeably hearty in this man's bronzed face, a heartiness that seemed to extend to his loosely knotted neckerchief. But what completely won my
25 good-will was a picture of enviable loveliness painted on his left arm. It was the head of a woman with the body of a fish. Her flowing hair was of livid green, and she held a pink comb in one hand. I never saw anything so beautiful. I determined to know that man. I think I would have given my brass pistol to have had such a picture painted on my arm.

In the middle of the stream we swung round, the current caught us, and away we flew
30 like a great winged bird. Only it didn't seem as if we were moving. The shore, with the countless steamboats, the tangled rigging of the ships, and the long lines of warehouses, appeared to be gliding away from us.

It was grand sport to stand on the quarter-deck and watch all this. Before long there was nothing to be seen on other side but stretches of low swampy land, covered with stunted
35 cypress trees, from which drooped delicate streamers of Spanish moss—a fine place for

Copyright Protected

alligators and Congo snakes. Here and there we passed a yellow sand-bar, and here and there a snag lifted its nose out of the water like a shark.

"This is your last chance to see the city, to see the city, Tom," said my father, as we swept round a bend of the river. I turned and looked. New Orleans was just a colorless mass
40 of something in the distance, and the dome of the St. Charles Hotel, upon which the sun shimmered for a moment, was no bigger than the top of old Aunt Chloe's thimble.

The ship seemed quite proud of being left to take care of itself, and, with its huge white sails bulged out, strutted off like a vain turkey. I had been standing by my father near the wheel-house all this while, observing things with that nicety of perception which belongs
45 only to children; but now the dew began falling, and we went below to have supper.

The fresh fruit and milk, and the slices of cold chicken, looked very nice; yet somehow I had no appetite. There was a general smell of tar about everything. Then the ship gave sudden lurches that made it a matter of uncertainty whether one was going to put his fork to his mouth or into his eye. The tumblers and wineglasses, stuck in a rack over the
50 table, kept clinking and clinking; and the cabin lamp, suspended by four gilt chains from the ceiling, swayed to and fro crazily. Now the floor seemed to rise, and now it seemed to sink under one's feet like a feather-bed.

There were not more than a dozen passengers on board, including ourselves; and all of these, excepting a bald-headed old gentleman—a retired sea-captain—disappeared into
55 their staterooms at an early hour of the evening.

After supper was cleared away, my father and the elderly gentleman, whose name was Captain Truck, played at checkers; and I amused myself for a while by watching the trouble they had in keeping the men in the proper places. Just at the most exciting point of the game, the ship would careen, and down would go the white checkers pell-mell
60 among the black. Then my father laughed, but Captain Truck would grow very angry, and vow that he would have won the game in a move or two more, if the confounded old chicken-coop—that's what he called the ship—hadn't lurched.

"I-I think I will go to bed now, please," I said, laying my hand on my father's knee, and feeling exceedingly strange.

65 It was high time, for the Typhoon was plunging about in the most alarming fashion.
I was speedily tucked away in the upper berth, where I felt a trifle more easy at first.
My clothes were placed on a narrow shelf at my feet, and it was a great comfort to me to know that my pistol was so handy, for I made no doubt we should fall in with Pirates before many hours. This is the last thing I remember with any distinctness. At midnight,
70 as I was afterwards told, we were struck by a gale which never left us until we came in sight of the Massachusetts coast.

For days and days I had no sensible idea of what was going on around me. That we were being hurled somewhere upside-down, and that I didn't like it, was about all I knew.
I have, indeed, a vague impression that my father used to climb up to the berth and call
75 me his "Ancient Mariner," bidding me cheer up. But the Ancient Mariner was far from cheering up, if I recollect rightly; and I don't believe that venerable navigator would have cared much if it had been announced to him, through a speaking-trumpet, that "a low, black, suspicious craft, with raking masts, was rapidly bearing down upon us!"

—*Anonymous*

28. From the opening line of this passage, we can **best** determine that the narrator
   A. is a reliable narrator
   B. is an unreliable narrator
   C. will not actually tell the whole story
   D. does not have a good memory

29. The description of the ship's feeling of pride at its independence is an example of
   A. simile
   B. hyperbole
   C. onomatopoeia
   D. personification

30. Captain Truck thinks he would have won the checkers game already, if
   A. the ship had not been hit with a wave
   B. he remembered how to play checkers
   C. he had not felt sick from the rolling seas
   D. the narrator's father had not laughed at him

31. The **best** explanation for why the narrator fears they will "fall in with Pirates" (line 68) is
   A. he is sick and therefore imagining things
   B. he is young and has an active imagination
   C. this part of the seas are infested with Pirates
   D. the captain has sent him to bed because the Pirates are very dangerous

32. The narrator **most likely** feels sick because he
   A. he feels homesick
   B. he has an upset stomach
   C. he has not been on the sea very much
   D. he ate something in the food that made him ill

33. From the passage, we can infer that the narrator does not clearly remember his father's calling him an "Ancient Mariner" (line 75) because
   A. he was sick in bed
   B. his memory is not very good
   C. he remembers only important events
   D. his father only told him later what he had done

34. This narrative is recounted in the

A. first person

B. second person

C. second person plural

D. third person

Read the following passage to answer questions 35 to 41.

LETTERS FROM ENGLAND 1846–1849

LETTER: TO W.D.B. AND A.B.

LIVERPOOL, October 26, 1846

My dear sons:

Thank God with me that we are once more on *TERRA FIRMA*. We arrived yesterday
5 morning at ten o'clock, after a very rough voyage and after riding all night in the Channel
in a tremendous gale, so bad that no pilot could reach us to bring us in on Saturday
evening. A record of a sea voyage will be only interesting to you who love me, but I
must give it to you that you may know what to expect if you ever undertake it; but first,
I must sum it all up by saying that of all horrors, of all physical miseries, tortures, and
10 distresses, a sea voyage is the greatest….

The Liverpool paper this morning, after announcing our arrival says: "The GREAT
WESTERN, notwithstanding she encountered throughout a series of most severe gales,
accomplished the passage in sixteen days and twelve hours."

To begin at the moment I left New York: I was so absorbed by the pain of parting
15 from you that I was in a state of complete apathy with regard to all about me. I did
not sentimentalize about "the receding shores of my country;" I hardly looked at them,
indeed. Friday I was awoke in the middle of the night by the roaring of the wind and sea
and SUCH motion of the vessel.

The gale lasted all Saturday and Sunday, strong from the North, and as we were in the
20 region where the waters of the Bay of Fundy run out and meet those of the Gulf of
St. Lawrence, afterwards we had a strong cross sea. May you never experience a "cross
sea." … Oh how I wished it had pleased God to plant some little islands as resting-
places in the great waste of waters, some resting station. But no, we must keep on, on,
with everything in motion that your eye could rest on. Everything tumbling about … we
25 lived through it, however, and the sun of Sunday morn rose clear and bright. A pilot got
on board about seven and at ten we were in Liverpool.

We are at the Adelphi. Before I had taken off my bonnet Mr. Richard Rathbone, one of
the wealthiest merchants here, called to invite us to dine the next day …. Mrs. Richard
Rathbone has written that beautiful "Diary of Lady Willoughby," and, what is more,
30 they say it is a perfect reflect of her own lovely life and character. When she published
the book no one knew of it but her husband, not even her brothers and sisters, and, of
course, she constantly heard speculations as to the authenticity of the book, and was often
appealed to for her opinion. She is very unpretending and sweet in her manners; talks
little, and seems not at all like a literary lady.

Not for Reproduction

35 I like these people in Liverpool. They seem to me to think less of fashion and more of substantial excellence than our wealthy people. I am not sure but the existence of a higher class above them has a favorable effect, by limiting them in some ways. There is much less show of furniture in the houses than with us, though their servants and equipages are in much better keeping. I am not sorry to be detained here for a few days

40 by my illness to become acquainted with them, and I think your father likes it also, and will find it useful to him. Let me say, while I think of it, how much I was pleased with the GREAT WESTERN. That upper saloon with the air passing through it was a great comfort to me. The captain, the servants, the table, are all excellent. Everything on board was as nice as in the best hotel, and my gruels and broths beautifully made. One

45 of the stewardesses did more for me than I ever had done by any servant of my own.... Your father and Louisa were ill but three or four days, and then your father read Tacitus and talked to the ladies, while Louisa played with the other children.

The Adelphi, my first specimen of an English hotel, is perfectly comfortable, and though an immense establishment, is quiet as a private house. There is none of the bustle of

50 the Astor[1], and if I ring my bedroom bell it is answered by a woman who attends to me assiduously. The landlord pays us a visit every day to know if we have all we wish.

LONDON, Sunday, November 1

Here I am in the mighty heart, but before I say one word about it I will go on from Wednesday evening with my journal. On Thursday, though still very feeble, I dined

55 at Green Bank, the country-seat of Mr. Richard Rathbone. I was unwilling to leave Liverpool without sharing with your father some of the hospitalities offered to us and made a great effort to go. The place is very beautiful and the house full of comfortable elegance.

The next morning we started for Birmingham, ninety-seven miles from Liverpool, on our

60 way to London, as I am unable to travel the whole way in a day. On this railway I felt for the first time the superiority of England to our own country. The cars are divided into first, second, and third classes. We took a first-class car, which has all the comforts of a private carriage.

Just as we entered Birmingham I observed the finest seat, surrounded by a park wall and

65 with a very picturesque old church, that I had seen on the way. On enquiring of young Mr. Van Wart, who came to see us in Birmingham (the nephew of Washington Irving), whose place it was, he said it was now called Aston Hall and was owned by Mr. Watt, but it was formerly owned by the Bracebridges, and was the veritable "Bracebridge Hall," and that his uncle had passed his Christmas there.

70 On arriving here we found our rooms all ready for us at Long's Hotel, kept by Mr. Markwell, a wine merchant. The house is in New Bond Street, in the very centre of movement at the West End, and Mr. Markwell full of personal assiduity, which we never see with us. He comes to the carriage himself, gives me his arm to go upstairs, is so much obliged to us for honoring his house, ushers you in to dinner, at least on the first

75 day, and seats you, etc., etc.

---

[1] the Astor—an elegant and expensive hotel in New York

Copyright Protected

Do not imagine us in fresh, new looking rooms as we should be in New York or Philadelphia. No, in London even new things look old, but almost everything IS old. Our parlor has three windows down to the floor, but it is very dark. The paint is maple color, and everything is dingy in appearance. The window in my bedroom looks like

80 a horn lantern, so thick is the smoke, and yet everything is scrupulously clean. On our arrival, Boyd, the Secretary of Legation, soon came, and stayed to dine with us at six. Our dinner was an excellent soup, the boiled cod garnished with fried smelts, the roast beef and a FRICANDEAU with sweet breads, then a pheasant, and afterwards, dessert.

—Anonymous

35. Which of the following statements **best** explains why the narrator likes the people from Liverpool?

A. They know how to dress.

B. They appreciate people with character.

C. They are hard-working, unlike her sons.

D. They look swarthy from all of the hard work.

36. From the context of the passage, the word "assiduously" (line 51) **most likely** means

A. lovingly

B. carefully

C. caustically

D. sarcastically

37. The narrator is journeying from the

A. Bay of Fundy to London

B. city of New York to Liverpool

C. Eastern Seaboard to Birmingham

D. St. Lawrence Seaway to the coast of Great Britain

38. Birmingham is _____ miles from Liverpool.

A. seventy-nine

B. ninety

C. ninety-seven

D. ninety-nine

39. The "seat" spotted by the narrator once she arrives in Birmingham is a

    A. place

    B. chair

    C. country estate

    D. park bench

40. The narrator's use of the phrase "at least not on the first day" (lines 74 to 75) implies that she

    A. thinks the superior service will soon stop

    B. thinks the service will continue indefinitely

    C. has paid a lot for the services of the bellhop

    D. believes this service is an example for her sons to follow

41. Which of the following phrases **most completely** explains the effect of the *epistolary narrative*?

    A. It serves no particular purpose in the story.

    B. It gives the reader a bird's-eye-view of the events.

    C. It gives the reader a feeling of intimacy with the narrator.

    D. It permits the writer to use more literary devices to get his point across.

Read the following passage to answer questions 42 to 48.

SONNET CXXX

My mistress' eyes are nothing like the sun;
Coral is far more red, than her lips red:
If snow be white, why then her breasts are dun[1];
If hairs be wires, black wires grow on her head.
5   I have seen roses damask'd, red and white,
But no such roses see I in her cheeks;
And in some perfumes is there more delight
Than in the breath that from my mistress reeks.
I love to hear her speak, yet well I know
10 That music hath a far more pleasing sound:
I grant I never saw a goddess go,—
My mistress, when she walks, treads on the ground:
And yet by heaven, I think my love as rare,
As any she belied with false compare.

—*by* William Shakespeare

[1] dun—the dull colour of a mouse

Copyright Protected

42. The speaker's comparison of his mistress' eyes with the sun is called a

    A. simile

    B. metaphor

    C. comparison

    D. juxtaposition

43. According to the speaker, both coral and roses are

    A. more lively looking than his mistress

    B. a deeper colour than his mistress's eyes

    C. redder than the lips and cheeks of his friend

    D. a deeper red than the lips and cheeks of his mistress

44. The meaning of the speaker's description of his mistress' hair is that it

    A. looks like wires to him

    B. has lots of bends and curls

    C. has a perm that holds it in place

    D. is exceptionally thick and full

45. The word "treads" (line 12) emphasizes that his mistress

    A. is not very graceful

    B. walks on the ground

    C. cannot jump very high

    D. is not a very fast runner

46. The statement that **best** describes the sonnet form is that it

    A. is a short poem of 16 lines

    B. expresses the speaker's feelings about his mistress

    C. has fourteen lines and closes with a rhyming couplet

    D. is a complicated poem that uses imagery, symbolism, and rhyme

47. The **main** purpose of the rhyming couplet is to

    A. rhyme the last words of both lines

    B. close the poem in a way the reader will remember

    C. contrast the speaker's mistress with different elements of nature

    D. contrast the speaker's feelings with his observations that were described above

48. One theme of this poem could be **best** described as the speaker

    A. wishes his mistress were more beautiful

    B. is simply introducing his mistress to the reader

    C. has a love that does not depend on superficial things like beauty

    D. realizes how much love actually depends on the attractiveness of his mistress

Read the following passage to answer questions 49 to 53.

WASTELANDS

If the reader will excuse me, I will say nothing of the circumstances which led me to leave my native country; the narrative would be tedious to him and painful to myself. Suffice it, that when I left home it was with the intention of going to some new colony, and either finding, or even perhaps purchasing, waste crown land suitable for cattle or
5 sheep farming, by which means I thought that I could better my fortunes more rapidly than in England. It will be seen that I did not succeed in my design, and that however much I may have met with that was new and strange, I have been unable to reap any financial advantage.

It is true, I imagine myself to have made a discovery which, if I can be the first to profit
10 by it, will bring me a recompense beyond all money computation, and secure me a position such as has not been attained by more than some fifteen or sixteen persons, since the creation of the universe. But to this end I must possess myself of a considerable sum of money: neither do I know how to get it, except by interesting the public in my story, and inducing the charitable to come forward and assist me. With this hope I now
15 publish my adventures; but I do so with great reluctance, for I fear that my story will be doubted unless I tell the whole of it; and yet I dare not do so, lest others with more means than mine should get the start of me. I prefer the risk of being doubted to that of being anticipated, and have therefore concealed my destination on leaving England, as also the point from which I began my more serious and difficult journey.

20 I reached my destination in one of the last months of 1868, but I dare not mention the season, lest the reader should gather in which hemisphere I was. The colony was one which had not been opened up even to the most adventurous settlers for more than eight or nine years, having been previously uninhabited, save by a few tribes of savages who frequented the seaboard. The part known to Europeans consisted of a coast-line about
25 eight hundred miles in length (affording three or four good harbours), and a tract of country extending inland for a space varying from two to three hundred miles, until it reached the offshoots of an exceedingly lofty range of mountains, which could be seen from far out upon the plains, and were covered with perpetual snow. The coast was perfectly well known both north and south of the tract to which I have alluded, but in
30 neither direction was there a single harbour for five hundred miles, and the mountains, which descended almost into the sea, were covered with thick timber, so that none would think of settling.

With this bay of land, however, the case was different. The harbours were sufficient; the country was timbered, but not too heavily; it was admirably suited for agriculture;
35 it also contained millions on millions of acres of the most beautifully grassed country in the world, and of the best suited for all manner of sheep and cattle. The climate was temperate, and very healthy; there were no wild animals, nor were the natives dangerous, being few in number and of an intelligent tractable disposition.

Copyright Protected

It may be readily understood that when once Europeans set foot upon this territory they
40 were not slow to take advantage of its capabilities. Sheep and cattle were introduced,
and bred with extreme rapidity; men took up their 50,000 or 100,000 acres of country,
going inland one behind the other, till in a few years there was not an acre between the
sea and the front ranges which was not taken up, and stations either for sheep or cattle
were spotted about at intervals of some twenty or thirty miles over the whole country.
45 The front ranges stopped the tide of squatters for some little time; it was thought that
there was too much snow upon them for too many months in the year,—that the sheep
would get lost, the ground being too difficult for shepherding,—that the expense of
getting wool down to the ship's side would eat up the farmer's profits,—and that the
grass was too rough and sour for sheep to thrive upon; but one after another determined
50 to try the experiment, and it was wonderful how successfully it turned out. Men pushed
farther and farther into the mountains, and found a very considerable tract inside the
front range, between it and another which was loftier still, though even this was not the
highest, the great snowy one which could be seen from out upon the plains. This second
range, however, seemed to mark the extreme limits of pastoral country; and it was here,
55 at a small and newly founded station, that I was received as a cadet, and soon regularly
employed. I was then just twenty-two years old.

I was delighted with the country and the manner of life. It was my daily business to
go up to the top of a certain high mountain, and down one of its spurs on to the flat, in
order to make sure that no sheep had crossed their boundaries. I was to see the sheep,
60 not necessarily close at hand, nor to get them in a single mob, but to see enough of them
here and there to feel easy that nothing had gone wrong; this was no difficult matter, for
there were not above eight hundred of them; and, being all breeding ewes, they were
pretty quiet.

There were a good many sheep which I knew, as two or three black ewes, and a black
65 lamb or two, and several others which had some distinguishing mark whereby I could tell
them. I would try and see all these, and if they were all there, and the mob looked large
enough, I might rest assured that all was well. It is surprising how soon the eye becomes
accustomed to missing twenty sheep out of two or three hundred. I had a telescope and
a dog, and would take bread and meat and tobacco with me. Starting with early dawn, it
70 would be night before I could complete my round; for the mountain over which I had to
go was very high. In winter it was covered with snow, and the sheep needed no watching
from above. If I were to see sheep dung or tracks going down on to the other side of the
mountain (where there was a valley with a stream), I was to follow them, and look out for
sheep; but I never saw any, the sheep always descending on to their own side, partly from
75 habit, and partly because there was abundance of good sweet feed, which had been burnt
in the early spring, just before I came, and was now deliciously green and rich, while that
on the other side had never been burnt, and was rank and coarse.

It was a monotonous life, but it was very healthy and one does not much mind anything when one is well. The country was the grandest that can be imagined. How often have
80 I sat on the mountain side and watched the waving downs, with the two white specks of huts in the distance, and the little square of garden behind them; the paddock with a patch of bright green oats above the huts, and the yards and wool-sheds down on the flat below; all seen as through the wrong end of a telescope, so clear and brilliant was the air, or as upon a colossal model or map spread out beneath me. Beyond the downs
85 was a plain, going down to a river of great size, on the farther side of which there were other high mountains, with the winter's snow still not quite melted; up the river, which ran winding in many streams over a bed some two miles broad, I looked upon the second great chain, and could see a narrow gorge where the river retired and was lost. I knew that there was a range still farther back; but except from one place near the very top of
90 my own mountain, no part of it was visible: from this point, however, I saw, whenever there were no clouds, a single snow-clad peak, many miles away, and I should think about as high as any mountain in the world. Never shall I forget the utter loneliness of the prospect—only the little far-away homestead giving sign of human handiwork;—the vastness of mountain and plain, of river and sky; the marvellous atmospheric effects–
95 sometimes black mountains against a white sky, and then again, after cold weather, white mountains against a black sky—sometimes seen through breaks and swirls of cloud—and sometimes, which was best of all, I went up my mountain in a fog, and then got above the mist; going higher and higher, I would look down upon a sea of whiteness, through which would be thrust innumerable mountain tops that looked like islands.

100 I am there now, as I write; I fancy that I can see the downs, the huts, the plain, and the river-bed—that torrent pathway of desolation, with its distant roar of waters. Oh, wonderful! wonderful! so lonely and so solemn, with the sad grey clouds above, and no sound save a lost lamb bleating upon the mountain side, as though its little heart were breaking. Then there comes some lean and withered old ewe, with deep gruff voice and
105 unlovely aspect, trotting back from the seductive pasture; now she examines this gully, and now that, and now she stands listening with uplifted head, that she may hear the distant wailing and obey it. Aha! they see, and rush towards each other. Alas! they are both mistaken; the ewe is not the lamb's ewe, they are neither kin nor kind to one another, and part in coldness. Each must cry louder, and wander farther yet; may luck be
110 with them both that they may find their own at nightfall.

—*by* Samuel Butler

49. According to the narrator, his **main** motivation for embarking on a journey to this faraway land was that he

A. wanted to make some money

B. was interested in different cultures

C. needed to leave his home country

D. had some financial difficulties at home

50. The **most complete** summary of his feelings about the remote land he visited is it was
    A. monotonous and boring
    B. very foggy most of the time
    C. healthy and full of breath-taking scenery
    D. an exciting place to entertain

51. The usual amount of land taken by a single settler in this country was
    A. 25 000 to 50 000 square miles
    B. 50 000 to 100 000 square miles
    C. 25 000 to 50 000 acres
    D. 50 000 to 100 000 acres

52. The final scene between a lost lamb and an old ewe is something that he
    A. sees as he writes
    B. was told by another shepherd
    C. imagines in his mind as he writes
    D. cannot forget, even though now he is back at home

53. The literary term that **best** describes the scenes that the narrator viewed while going about his daily duties in the mountains is
    A. gothic
    B. pastoral
    C. sublime
    D. romantic

Read the following passage to answer questions 54 to 60.

YOU HAD TWO GIRLS

You had two girls—Baptiste—
One is Virginie—
Hold hard—Baptiste!
Listen to me.

5 The whole drive was jammed
In that bend at the Cedars,
The rapids were dammed
With the logs tight rammed
And crammed; you might know
10 The Devil had clinched them below.

We worked three days—not a budge,
'She's as tight as a wedge, on the ledge,'
Says our foreman;
'Mon Dieu! boys, look here,
15 We must get this thing clear.'
He cursed at the men
And we went for it then;
With our cant-dogs arow[1],
We just gave he-yo-ho;
20 When she gave a big shove
From above.

The gang yelled and tore
For the shore,
The logs gave a grind
25 Like a wolf's jaws behind,
And as quick as a flash,
With a shove and a crash,
They were down in a mash,
But I and ten more,

30 All but Isaàc Dufour,
Were ashore.
He leaped on a log in the front of the rush,
And shot out from the bind
While the jam roared behind;

35 As he floated along
He balanced his pole
And tossed us a song.
But just as we cheered,
Up darted a log from the bottom,

---

[1] cant-dogs arow—men with cant hooks all working on one
log to twist it free

Copyright Protected

40   Leaped thirty feet square and fair,
      And came down on his own.
      He went up like a block
      With the shock,
      And when he was there

45   In the air,
      Kissed his hand
      To the land;
      When he dropped
      My heart stopped,

50   For the first logs had caught him
      And crushed him;
      When he rose in his place
      There was blood on his face.
      There were some girls, Baptiste,

55   Picking berries on the hillside,
      Where the river curls, Baptiste,
      You know—on the still side
      One was down by the water,
      She saw Isaàc
60   Fall back.

      She did not scream, Baptiste,
      She launched her canoe;
      It did seem, Baptiste,
      That she wanted to die too,
65   For before you could think
      The birch cracked like a shell
      In that rush of hell,
      And I saw them both sink—

      Baptiste!—
70   He had two girls,
      One is Virginie,
      What God calls the other
      Is not known to me.

—*by* Duncan Campbell Scott

54. The repetition of sounds in the words "jammed," "dammed," "rammed," and "crammed," (stanza 2) emphasizes

A. the logger's view of the logs

B. how tightly the logs were stuck on the river

C. the sound the logs were making on the river

D. the speaker's frustration at not getting the logs free for three days

55. In the poem, the lightness of the verb "tossed" (line 37) as well as the simple rhyme of "along" with "song" (lines 35 and 37) contrasts with the

    A. cheers of the men on the shore

    B. silence of the woman in the canoe

    C. tragedy of his drowning an instant later

    D. horrible sound of the logs grinding behind him

56. The simile, that the girl's birch canoe "cracked like a shell" (line 66), helps us understand that

    A. shells tend to crack very easily

    B. she should not have followed Dufour into the water

    C. she did not know how to paddle a canoe to Dufour in those conditions

    D. it was easy for the powerful logs to snap her canoe in half

57. The speaker addresses a person by the name of "Baptiste" to whom he tells this story. The person's name is ironic because

    A. no baptism had been performed at that river

    B. Isaàc Dufour had not actually seen what had happened

    C. he was not part of the events in the poem

    D. Isaàc Dufour was baptized in a sense, though he never walked out of the water

58. The phrase that **best** describes the scene in the poem is

    A. loggers led a dangerous life

    B. the speaker addresses people by their names

    C. a man and a woman drown on the river

    D. a logjam becomes unstuck, but kills a logger and a woman

59. Line 1 addresses Baptiste with a second person singular pronoun "You" while line 70 uses the third person singular pronoun "He." This difference **most likely** indicates that

    A. Baptiste has left before the story could be finished

    B. the speaker has forgotten to whom he is speaking

    C. the speaker is talking about Baptiste who has drowned

    D. the speaker made a simple mistake

60. Symbolically, the speaker **probably** does not know the name of the other girl because she

    A. is the one who drowned

    B. was the bravest of the two

    C. becomes a more tragic figure by remaining nameless

    D. never told him her name before she went out in her canoe

Copyright Protected

Read the following passage to answer questions 61 to 67.

STARS

Now in the West the slender moon lies low,
And now Orion[1] glimmers through the trees,
Clearing the earth with even pace and slow,
And now the stately-moving Pleiades[2],
5 In that soft infinite darkness overhead
Hang jewel-wise upon a silver thread.

And all the lonelier stars that have their place,
Calm lamps within the distant southern sky,
And planet-dust upon the edge of space,
10 Look down upon the fretful world, and I
Look up to outer vastness unafraid
And see the stars which sang when earth was made.

—*by* Marjorie Pickthall

---

[1] Orion—constellation, taking the form of a hunter with a belt and a sword.

[2] Pleiades—the seven daughters of Atlas in Greek myth; and, a group of stars in the constellation Taurus, not far from Orion

---

61. The description of the "slender moon" as lying low (line 1) probably indicates that the moon

  A. was not full

  B. was about to set in the West

  C. was not in a vertical position

  D. was waning instead of waxing

62. The fact that the stars seem to be looking down on the earth, as the speaker looks up at them, may help explain why she

  A. feels so calm

  B. can hear the stars singing

  C. reads her horoscope every day

  D. does not feel afraid while looking up at them

63. The line "And see the stars which sang when earth was made" (line 12) contains an example of

  A. simile

  B. hyperbole

  C. onomatopoeia

  D. personification

64. The reference to the stars singing "when the earth was made" (line 12) emphasizes

    A. the vastness of both space and time the speaker feels

    B. sounds that she hears while seeing the stars

    C. a metaphor for light that is auditory

    D. the myths in which she believes

65. The form of this poem could **best** be described as

    A. *abab*

    B. *abba*

    C. *abcabc*

    D. *ababcc*

66. The **best** function of the rhyming couplet at the end of each verse is to

    A. rhyme in a "*cc*" pattern

    B. make the poem easier to remember

    C. contrast with the vast openness of the sky

    D. show what the speaker is thinking while she looks up at the sky

67. The sense that is represented **most strongly** in this poem is

    A. smell

    B. touch

    C. taste

    D. sight

ANSWERS AND SOLUTIONS—PRACTICE TEST 2

1. C	11. A	21. D	31. B	41. C	51. D	61. B
2. B	12. D	22. B	32. C	42. A	52. C	62. D
3. C	13. B	23. D	33. A	43. D	53. B	63. D
4. C	14. B	24. B	34. A	44. A	54. B	64. A
5. D	15. B	25. C	35. B	45. A	55. C	65. D
6. C	16. A	26. A	36. B	46. C	56. D	66. B
7. B	17. B	27. D	37. B	47. D	57. D	67. D
8. B	18. D	28. B	38. C	48. C	58. D	
9. A	19. B	29. D	39. C	49. A	59. A	
10. B	20. D	30. A	40. A	50. C	60. C	

1. C

According to the passage, the responsibility of raising Emma was left to Miss Taylor, the governess that her father hired. The other selections are not reflected in this text and therefore are not satisfactory responses.

2. B

From the context of the passage, you know that Miss Taylor was a governess in name only. This figure of speech does not indicate that she did not fulfill her duties as governess for Emma, but on the contrary, fulfilled them well beyond the call of duty. Although "to nominate" also has the same root meaning of "to name," to nominate someone would involve placing their name in a public forum where they could be voted into public office.

3. C

Emma's situation is fraught with evil because she has gotten used to having her own way. Since she was raised by an attentive and doting governess, with no other siblings to interact with, Emma had not had her wishes denied very many times. The fact that the narrator considers this situation "fraught with evil" is not a hyperbolic statement on the narrator's part, but rather reflects the popular thinking of the time regarding child-raising and character building.

4. C

The nearly unbearable change experienced by Emma at the outset of this narrative, does not point to the "evils" mentioned in solution two. Instead it suggests the intimacy of her relation with her governess, Miss Taylor. Although the position of governess was one that received a wage, you can see something of Miss Taylor's own character qualities in how conscientiously she approached her duties. The narrative focuses on Emma's response to this situation instead of the governess's. You are not allowed to know Miss Taylor's own feelings as she left Emma and her father's home.

5. D

The last sentence of the first paragraph provides the information that you need to correctly answer this question. Although the sentence indicates that Emma was nearly twenty-one years of age, this answer is closer to any of the others that are offered and thus must be the best response.

6. C

The narrator states that Mr. Weston was "a man of unexceptionable character, easy fortune, suitable age, and pleasant manners…" The passage does indicate that he was "relaxed," but not that he was lazy. Physical fitness does not reflect on Mr. Weston's character and thus cannot be considered as a response here.

Copyright Protected

7. B

In the second-last paragraph the narrator states that Emma's father was not good company for her because "he was no companion for her. He could not meet her in conversation, rational or playful." Although his responsibilities managing the estate may have prevented him from engaging in witty repartee with his daughter, the narrator's perspective is the one you must take into account in order to select the correct response. The narrator's use of "intellectual solitude" suggests emotional and mental deprivation for Emma.

8. B

Miss Hilaria may not be able to forget about "that Valentine", and she may metaphorically have him "in" her head. But the reason why she is unable to forget him derives from the love she feels for him. Thus the second distractor is the best response.

9. A

According to the passage, Lord Exbury is obliged to move into more humble quarters. The reasons that are offered involve his son Morduant's excessive debts, not any expenses that were mounted by Valentine.

10. B

Since you recognize that Hilaria has formed an attachment with Valentine, it is easy for you to infer from her statement, "I am undone," that she "fears she will not be able to live with Lord Exbury's family anymore", thus forfeiting an opportunity to enjoy a future with Valentine. This fear, at this point, is greater than the other one she experienced only seconds earlier, that her "attraction to Valentine will be discovered by Lord Exbury".

11. A

Although Hilaria seems to feel that her love for Valentine may be found out through her conversation with Lord Exbury, these asides let us hear her thoughts about this danger and her feelings about the impending move. The effect of these asides in fact draws the audience closer to Hilaria instead of creating distance. They have no noticeable effect on the audience's feelings of sympathy for Lord Exbury.

12. D

Lord Exbury saves Morduant from his creditors by paying off the debt with the sale of his estate. The other responses do not reflect the value of Lord Exbury's action and therefore can be discarded.

13. B

To state that Hilaria has an "attachment" to Valentine, based on your insight into her thoughts about him, is an example of understatement. None of the other responses reflect her feelings of love for Valentine.

14. B

Uberto tells Osmond that he has come some distance from the hunting party, where they were chasing a wild boar. The passage does state that Uberto has nearly been killed by a boar, but stating "In my life shall I never forget …" suggests that it happened earlier. We might infer that he was excited to speak with Osmond, or that he had been thinking about Constantia just before meeting Osmond. None of these options reflect the evidence given explicitly in the text, and therefore must be discounted.

15. B

According to Uberto, Sigismond is a hero because he "advanced, brandished his spear with a determined look—as—thus!—and—I will not wrong my honesty so far as to say I saw him kill the monster—But this I will certify—I saw the monster dead, and heard our whole troop shout to the honour of Sigismond." Although Uberto does not actually see Sigismond kill the boar, the narrative offers other corroborative evidence, such as the troop's shout in honour of Sigismond.

16. A

You do not meet Sigismond directly in this excerpt, but based on the conversation between Osmond and Uberto you can surmise that he is brave, for his role in killing the wild boar that might have killed Uberto. The evidence contradicts that he is cowardly and a clown. That he is handsome is not mentioned in this passage and thus can be ruled out.

17. B

The main meaning of Osmond's statement, "He had ne'er been a prisoner but in the cause of the Count," is that Sigismond was sent to prison as a result of performing some duty on behalf of the Count. The implication is that Sigismond himself did not deserve to be sent to prison, but was punished for his unwitting involvement in another person's crime. Although he may have therefore been innocent and was unfairly punished, the more specific answer is the one that most successfully responds to the question.

18. D

Osmond tells Uberto that "on the day my lord and his daughter were taken captive by a band of wandering Poles—this young stranger—this valiant Sigismond, stood forth to save her from dishonour, and drew his sabre even against his countrymen." None of the other responses offered here reflects the action that Sigismond took in defending Constantia from her would-be kidnappers.

19. B

Although it appears that Sigismond is trying to win Constantia's heart, the main meaning of Osmond's speech to Uberto is not that they were made for each other, nor even that Constantia has not noticed Sigismond, but indignation that Sigismond who is not of a royal blood, should think himself worthy of her affections.

20. D

In literature the metaphor of the 'hunt' often represents the pursuit and capture of a beloved by a lover. Although this metaphor today may be distasteful, implying a certain violence and resistance in the chase on the part of the beloved, at the time of this narrative, the simultaneity of the description could indeed be intended to comment on the similarities of one pastime with the other.

21. D

Maurice Hilliard tells Mrs. Hilliard that he has received a cheque that covered a debt owed his father by a gentleman named Dengate. You can safely infer, from this passage, that Maurice's receipt of this money is responsible for his sharp change in demeanor. The passage does not state why Maurice feels at liberty to disburse money owed to his father, but the fact remains that it was not directly owed to him.

22. B

The literary technique represented here is known as "metaphor" since it compares Dengate with the unsavoury qualities of a reptile. Since the comparison does not use "like" or "as" you know that it could not be a simile. You also know that hyperbole involves the use of exaggeration to create rhetorical effects. Furthermore, personification gives human qualities to inanimate objects.

23. D

This question also asks you to identify some factual information from the passage. Once you have found this information you can safely disregard the other responses that the question offers. You might think that Maurice could have been afraid, wanting to run, or prevented from getting the money. Maurice specifically tells Mrs. Hilliard that he would have strangled him with everyone watching.

24. B

Mrs. Hilliard is reluctant to accept Maurice's offer of financial support because she feels that she has been a "burden" to him already. The final statement in the passage implies that she does indeed need the money that he offers, and that she has no other grounds on which to resist the offer he is making. She knows that she has his affections already, therefore ruling out this condition as a factor.

25. C

The strange news that she tells Maurice regards her marriage to Ezra Marr. This marriage does not involve eloping, nor her having received money.

26. A

The narrator explains that Mrs. Hilliard feels reluctant to tell Maurice that she is marrying Ezra Marr because he comes from a labourers' class. Since he is so different from Maurice's family, Mrs. Hilliard attempts to describe him in as favourable a light as possible.

27. D

As the solution above states, Mrs. Hilliard's initial reluctance was not based on her improved financial standing, but on her reluctance to burden Maurice further.

28. B

You know that he will not be a reliable narrator because he tells about the illness he suffered while on this voyage. The evidence thus contradicts that he is a reliable narrator. His memory on the whole may be really quite sharp. He does not tell the whole story as a result of illness. However, this response implies that he knows more than he is telling, and inference that is also undermined by evidence from the text.

29. D

Attributing human characteristics to inanimate objects, such as ships, is known as "personification".

30. A

Captain Truck feels angry because the lurching ship causes the checker pieces to fall onto the floor, thus prolonging the game and preventing him from beating the narrator's father. From this information, you know that Captain Truck himself does not feel sick, as does the narrator. You also know that the Captain feels quite confident of his checker-playing abilities.

31. B

The narrative does not indicate that these waters carry any threats from Pirates. The narrator may have imagined the Pirate threat as a result of his illness; however, the evidence from the text does not link the narrator's illness with his imaginings.

32. C

The narrator states that the sea was "plunging about in the most alarming fashion." From this evidence you can infer that it was the sea, and not the food, nor loneliness, nor illness that was laying him low.

33. A

The "vagueness" of the narrator's recollections derive from the illness he was suffering. The illness itself has no bearing on the functioning of his memory in general. The text does not state that his father told him this information later, allowing you to rule this answer out as well.

34. A

The clue that a narrative is told in the first person singular is the use of "I." If the narrator is reporting events that happened to him or her, you can safely select "first person" as the correct response. A second person narration would be indicated with the use of "you," in either singular or plural. Third person narration is another conventional narrative technique. Third person narration offers the "bird's eye view" of the narrative events.

35. B

The narrator writes that she likes "these people in Liverpool. They seem to me to think less of fashion and more of substantial excellence than our wealthy people." This evidence undermines the intentions of "they know how to dress," and "they look swarthy from all of the hard work." The letters do not indicate that the sons have any aversion to hard work.

36. B

The narrator comments on the service that she receives from the staff at the hotel at which she is staying. Since "loving" care would not seem appropriate for hotel staff attending on clients, and since sarcastic or caustic comments would not earn a favorable report, the only response left us is "carefully". Thus by the process of elimination we are able to determine the correct answer, even if we had never seen the word "assiduously" before.

37. B

To discover the correct answer to this question, you need to read through the passage and piece the answer together. When the narrator informs her sons of where they departed from, she states that it was New York. Later she states that they arrived in Liverpool. Therefore this is the only response that could be correct.

38. C

The passage informs you that the distance from Birmingham to Liverpool is ninety-seven miles.

39. C

A more obscure meaning of "seat" is country estate. In this historical context, this would be the meaning intended by the narrator.

40. A

Of the answers offered here, "she thinks the superior service may soon stop" most accurately reflects the meaning of the phrase excerpted from the narrative. If she had thought the service may continue indefinitely, or that she believes that her payment of services to the bellhop would cause the service to continue, the narrator would not have expressed some doubt as to the length of time this superior service would continue. The narrator does not explicitly state that her sons should follow the example of the hotel staff.

41. C

A "bird's-eye-view" of events would not be written in an epistolary form, since this form would only offer the perspective of the author of the letters. Since each literary form permits the author to utilize certain literary devices to make the writing as effective as possible, and each form does in fact serve some particular purpose, you can safely rule out either of these alternatives as possible responses. The reader does gain a deeper sense of intimacy with the narrator in an epistolary narrative, because you can understand the narrator's thoughts and impressions directly from his or her writing, without the mediation of another narrator's report.

42. A

Although a metaphor is also a term that describes the juxtaposition of two unlike objects, a simile is a comparison that uses "like" or "as."

43. D

The strongest answer is the one that is the most specific. Although the narrator thinks that both coral and roses look more beautiful that his friend's lips and cheeks, the more specific response is that coral and roses are a deeper red than the lips and cheeks of his mistress.

44. A

The intent of the speaker's description of his mistress is to show that he does not think she is attractive by conventional standards. Although each of the other responses might be true on some level, the only one that reflects the intent of the speaker in describing her in this way is "her hair looks like wires."

45. A

The word "treads" must be read in the context within which it is used to help you determine the emphasis that this sonnet is placing on it. Although the term literally may refer to her way of walking, in fact this reference comments on his mistress's lack of gracefulness in general.

46. C

Discovering the correct response to this question requires selecting the distractor that applies exclusively to the sonnet form. The first selection is incorrect, since a sonnet contains fourteen lines instead of sixteen. The last statement is too broad to be of use here, since many poems use imagery, symbolism and rhyme. While it is correct to say that this particular sonnet expresses the speaker's feelings about his mistress, not all sonnets serve this purpose. The correct response describes the basic structure of a sonnet.

Copyright Protected

47. D

The couplet does close with a rhyme that helps the reader remember the meaning of the poem. However, the answer that most specifically summarizes the *main* purpose of the couplet in this particular sonnet is "contrast the speaker's feelings with his observations that were described above."

48. C

The opening two words of the rhyming couplet give the reader a clue that he does not think his feelings of love for his mistress are determined by superficial things like beauty. The words signal a shift from the direction of the twelve lines that have come before: "And yet…" The speaker contrasts his description of his mistress with the intense feelings he holds for her.

49. A

In the opening paragraph, the narrator states that he purchased land in this remote place because he hoped to make his fortune from raising sheep.

50. C

Although the narrator does state that he found the life in this remote land to be monotonous, the better answer to this question is the one that acknowledges the effect that this monotony had on him. He states that the rest from the busyness of the city was beneficial to his health.

51. D

The narrator states that a single settler usually purchased between 50,000 and 100,000 acres of land.

52. C

At the beginning of the paragraph the narrator states that he is "there" as he writes the passage that you are reading. Is he literally "there"? In the sentence that follows, he states that he "fancies" being able to see the scenery from that country-side. Therefore, any answer that fails to acknowledge the fact that he imagines the scenario that he describes could not be a successful response.

53. B

The calm natural scenery may seem like an appropriate setting for a romance. However, the term that is commonly applied to these kind of scenes is the "pastoral", since they depict natural vistas seen from a distance, without storms brewing on the horizon. A gothic scene, on the other hand, may contain elements that seem ominous or sinister, with shadows, moonlight and unidentifiable noises. A sublime scene is the name given to natural phenomena that may both terrify and thrill, such as intense storms or dangerously high and sharp cliffs.

54. B

This verse describes not the sound of the logs on the river, nor the speaker's frustration at not getting the logs free. The verse does describe, however, the tightly stuck logs themselves. Although the repetition of these sounds offers us an example of internal rhyme, these sounds emphasize the meaning of the words, instead of the technique itself.

55. C

The lightness of Dufour's song emphasizes his playful celebration of the freeing of the logs. This celebration contrasts with the tragedy of his drowning an instant later as he is thrown into the mass of grinding logs around him. This response most directly addresses the central event of the poem and thus is the only correct answer you could select.

56. D

The quick sharp sound of the word "cracked" emphasizes the ease with which the heavy log snapped her canoe in half. Although this event implies that she should not have followed Dufour into the water, nor perhaps that she did not understand how to paddle a canoe in those conditions, the best response is the one that refers most specifically to the event that is described.

57. D

The term "irony" applies to words whose context causes them to take on meanings that are the opposite of their literal dictionary definitions. The irony in this poem applies to Dufour's drowning. Dufour is submerged beneath the water as takes place at a baptism. However, ironically Dufour does not walk out of the water after this baptism.

58. D

The phrase that *best* describes the scene in this poem is the one that most specifically identifies the elements in this particular event. A man and a woman do drown on the river in this poem, the speaker does address someone named "Baptiste", and loggers did lead a dangerous life. However, the events that take place in this particular poem are "a logjam becomes unstuck, but kills a logger and a woman."

59. A

This type of question requires you to infer a correct response based on the information that is presented in the poem. You can assume the intentionality of the speaker. You can also assume that the subject of the speaker's narrative would not influence the person in which he decides to tell the story. Thus, although you are not told directly that Baptiste has left the scene of this telling and this accident, you can assume that this is the case based on the evidence presented in the poem.

60. C

You are asked to weigh the symbolic significance of the fact that the drowned girl is not given a name in this poem. If you compare her situation with Dufour's (who drowns, but is identified in the poem), this contrast heightens the sense of tragedy and waste in the drowning of this girl.

61. B

The speaker tells you that the moon lies low in the Western sky. From this information you can infer that the moon is about to set. None of the other responses can be inferred from this information, and therefore must be disregarded as possible answers for the question.

62. D

Although the speaker does seem to feel calm as she looks up at the stars, "does not feel afraid" more specifically repeats the author's own word to describe her feelings.

63. D

The personification of Orion and Pleiades does show how much these constellations are like people moving slowly.

64. A

To select the correct response to this question, you need to be aware of the context within which these words are expressed. Throughout the poem the speaker notices the grandeur and stateliness of the stars that slowly pass by overhead. This grandeur leads her to feel calm and unafraid despite the fretfulness of the world around her. You can see that the calming influence of the stars derives from her perception of the stars as existing in another realm that moves slowly and is much more stable than her own. The only response that underscores the speaker's sense is the speaker's awareness of "the vastness of both space and time."

65. D

The first four lines do close with an "*abab*" rhyming pattern. However, this answer does not recognize an important shift in the rhyme scheme in lines 5 and 6.

66. B

You can discover the best answer here, through the process of elimination. Although the openness of the sky is one of the scenes that the poem describes, this description is not related directly to the rhyming couplets that conclude each verse. The rhyming couplets also do not show what the speaker is thinking when she looks up at the sky. Likewise, **A** fails because it describes what the rhyming couplet *is* without describing its function, as the question requests. The only answer that is left, is also correct enough to be successful: one of function of rhyming patterns is that they serve as mnemonic devices, or aids to memory.

67. D

The initial descriptions that the speaker offers as she stands under the skies at night are of the stars that are moving slowly overhead. Together with the speaker, you see the "slender moon," "Orion's glimmer" and the "stately-moving Pleiades." Evidence from the final stanza confirms that "sight" is your best response. The speaker states that the stars "Look down upon the fretful world." The speaker in turn "Look[s] up to outer vastness unafraid." Thus vision is the primary sense that is represented in the poem.

Copyright Protected

NOTES

Appendices

Copyright Protected

SOME COMMON LITERARY TERMS

Abstract	Abstract terms and concepts name things that are not knowable through the senses; examples are love, justice, guilt, and honour. See *concrete*.
Allegory	A story or visual image with a second distinct meaning partially hidden. It involves a continuous parallel between two or more levels of meaning so that its persons and events correspond to their equivalents in a system of ideas or chain of events external to the story.
Alliteration	Repetition of initial consonant sounds
Allusion	Indirect or passing reference to some person, place, or event; or to a piece of literature or art. The nature of the reference is not explained because the writer relies on the reader's familiarity with it.
Analogy	A comparison that is made to explain something that is unfamiliar by presenting an example that is similar or parallel to it in some significant way
Anecdote	A brief story of an interesting incident
Antecedent Action	Action that takes place before the story opens
Antithesis	A contrast or opposition of ideas; the second part of a statement that contrasts opposite ideas
Apathy	Lack of interest
Apostrophe	A speech addressed to a dead or absent person or to an inanimate object (Do not confuse this use of apostrophe with the punctuation mark.)
Archaic	Belonging to an earlier time; words or expressions that have passed out of use are said to be archaic
Aside	Comment made by an actor and supposedly not heard by other actors
Assonance	Repetition of similar or identical vowel sounds
Ballad	A narrative poem that tells a story, often in a straightforward and dramatic manner, and often about such universals as love, honour, and courage. Ballads were once songs. Literary ballads often have the strong rhythm and the plain rhyme schemes of songs. Songs are still written in ballad form, some old ballads are still sung, and some literary ballads have been set to music. Samuel Taylor Coleridge's "The Rime of the Ancient Mariner" is an example of a literary ballad.
Blank Verse	Poetry written in unrhymed iambic pentameters
Caricature	A distorted representation to produce a comic or ridiculous effect
Chronological	In order of time
Cliché	An overused expression; one that has become stale through overuse
Colloquial	Informal, suitable for everyday speech but not for formal writing
Concrete	A concrete thing exists in a solid, physical state, and is knowable through the senses; trees, copper, and kangaroos are all examples of concrete things. See *abstract*.
Connotation	Implied or additional meaning that a word or phrase imparts. Such meaning is often subjective. See also *denotation*.
Deduction	A conclusion reached by logic or reasoning, or by examining all the available information
Denotation	The explicit or direct meaning of a word or expression, aside from the impressions it creates. These are the meanings listed in dictionaries. See also *connotation*.
Discrepancy	Distinct difference between two things that should not be different, or that should correspond
Dissonance	Harsh sound or discordance; in poetry, a harsh jarring combination of sounds
Epic	A long poem that is often about a heroic character. The style is elevated and the poetry often represents religious or cultural ideals; the Iliad and the Odyssey are examples of epics
Epilogue	A final address to the audience, often delivered by a character in a drama
Fantasy	A literary genre; generally contains events, characters, or settings that would not be possible in real life
Foreshadowing	A storytelling technique; something early in the story hints at later events

Free Verse	Is usually written in variable rhythmic cadences; it may be rhymed or unrhymed, but the rhymes are likely to be irregular and may not occur at the end of lines
Hyperbole	A figure of speech that uses exaggeration for effect
Imagery	Language that evokes sensory impressions
Imitative Harmony	Words that seem to imitate the sounds to which they refer; buzz and whisper are examples of imitative harmony; also called *onomatopoeia*
Interior Monologue	Conversation-like thoughts of a character
Irony	The difference—in actions or words—between reality and appearance. Authors use irony for both serious and humorous effects. Irony can also be a technique for indicating, through character or plot development, the writer's own attitude toward some element of the story.
Jargon	Special vocabulary of a particular group or activity; sometimes used to refer to confusing or unintelligible language
Justification	The giving of reasons or support; for example, giving an argument or reason that shows that an action or belief is reasonable or true
Juxtaposition (or contrast)	The deliberate contrast of characters, settings, or situations for effect; the effect may be a demonstration of character or heightening of mood
Lyric	A poem that expresses the private emotions or thoughts of the writer; sonnets, odes, and elegies are examples of lyrics
Metamorphosis	An alteration in appearance or character
Metaphor	Comparison without using the words like or as
Metrical poetry	Is written in regular, repeating rhythms and may be rhymed or unrhymed; when rhymes are used, they are generally regular, like the rhythm, and are often found at the end of the line
Monologue	A literary form; an oral or written composition in which only one person speaks
Mood	In a story, the atmosphere; when a writer orders the setting, action, and characters of a story so as to suggest a dominant emotion or patterns of emotions, this emotional pattern is the mood of the story. Also a person's state of mind or complex of emotions at any given time
Motif	A recurring theme, situation, incident, idea, image, or character type that is found in literature
Ode	A poem expressing lofty emotion; odes often celebrate an event or are addressed to nature or to some admired person, place, or thing; an example is "Ode to a Grecian Urn" by John Keats
Onomatopoeia	Words that seem to imitate the sounds to which they refer. See also *imitative harmony*
Oxymoron	A combination of two usually contradictory terms in a compressed paradox; for example, "the living dead." An oxymoron is like a metaphor in that it expresses in words some truth that cannot be understood literally; truthful lies is an oxymoron that describes metaphors
Parable	A short, often simple story that teaches or explains a lesson—often a moral or religious lesson
Paradox	An apparently self-contradictory statement that is, in fact, true
Parallelism	The arrangement of similarly constructed clauses, verses, or sentences
Parenthetical	A word, phrase, or passage (sometimes within parentheses) that explains or modifies a thought
Personification	The giving of human attributes to objects or to abstract ideas
Prologue	An introduction to a play, often delivered by the chorus (in ancient Greece, a group, but in modern plays, one actor) who plays no part in the following action
Pun	A humorous expression that depends on a double meaning, either between different senses of the same word or between two similar sounding words
Rhetoric	The art of speaking or writing
Rhetorical Question	A question for which a reply is not required or even wanted; the question is asked for effect. Often, a rhetorical question is a way of making a statement: Is there anyone who does not believe in freedom? really means Everyone believes in freedom.
Ridicule	Contemptuous laughter or derision (contempt and mockery); ridicule may be an element of satire

Satire	A form of writing that exposes the failings of individuals, institutions, or societies to ridicule or scorn in order to correct or expose some evil or wrongdoing
Simile	Comparison using the words like or as
Soliloquy	A speech by a character who is alone on stage, or whose presence is unrecognized by the other characters; the purpose is to make the audience aware of the character's thoughts or to give information concerning other characters or about the action
Sonnet	A lyric poem fourteen lines long and usually written in iambic pentameter. The Shakespearean sonnet consists of three quatrains (four-line stanzas) and a couplet (two lines), all written to a strict end-rhyme scheme (abab cdcd efef gg). The development of the poet's thoughts is also structured. There are several methods: one method is to use each quatrain for different points in an argument and the couplet for the resolution of the argument. Because of the complexity of the sonnet, poets sometimes find it a suitable form for expressing the complexity of thought and emotion.
Symbol	Anything that stands for or represents something other than itself. In literature, a symbol is a word or phrase referring to an object, scene, or action that also has some further significance associated with it. For example, a rose is a common symbol of love. Many symbols, such as flags, are universally recognized. Other symbols are not so universally defined. They do not acquire a meaning until they are defined by how they are used in a story. They may even suggest more than one meaning. For example, snow might be used to symbolize goodness because of its cleanness, or cruelty because of its coldness.

Symbols are often contained in story titles; in character and place names; in classical, literary, and historical allusions and references; in images or figures that appear at important points in a story; and in images that either receive special emphasis or are repeated. |
| Thesis | A statement that is made as the first step in an argument or a demonstration |
| Tone | A particular way of speaking or writing. Tone may also describe the general feeling of a piece of work. It can demonstrate the writer's attitude toward characters, settings, conflicts, and so forth. The many kinds of tone include thoughtful, chatty, formal, tragic, or silly; tone can also be a complex mixture of attitudes. Different tones can cause readers to experience such varying emotions as pity, fear, horror, or humour. |

DIRECTING WORDS

The following list of directory words and definitions may help you plan your writing. For example, a particular discussion might include assessment, description, illustrations, or an outline of how an extended argument could be developed.

Directing Word	Definition
Agree Or Disagree	Support or contradict a statement; give the positive or negative features; express an informed opinion one way or the other; list the advantages for or against
Assess	Estimate the value of something based on some criteria; present an informed judgment. The word "assess" strongly suggests that two schools of thought exist about a given subject. Assessing usually involves weighing the relative merit of conflicting points of view; e.g., negative vs. positive, strong vs. weak components, long-range vs. short-term
Compare	Point out similarities or differences; describe the relationship between two things; often used in conjunction with contrast
Contrast	Show or emphasize differences when compared; see compare
Describe	Give a detailed or graphic account of an object, event, or sequence of events
Discuss	Present the various points of view in a debate or argument; write at length about a given subject; engage in written discourse on a particular topic
Explain	Give an account of what the essence of something is, how something works, or why something is the way it is; may be accomplished by paraphrasing, providing reasons or examples, or by giving a step-by-step account

Identify	Establish the identity of something; establish the unique qualities of something; provide the name of something
Illustrate	Give concrete examples to clarify; provide explanatory or decorative features
List	Itemize names, ideas, or things that belong to a particular class or group
Outline	Give a written description of only the main features; summarize the principal parts of a thing, an idea, or an event
Show (that)	Give facts, reasons, illustrations or examples, to support an idea or proposition
State	Give the key points; declare
Suggest	Propose alternatives, options, or solutions
Support	Defend or agree with a particular point of view; give evidence, reasons, or examples
Trace	Outline the development of something; describe a specified sequence

SOME EASILY CONFUSED WORDS

• a, an	• Both are articles. Use *a* before a consonant sound, *an* before a vowel sound	• a box, a unicorn, a hit • an apple, an historian, an heir
• accept • except	• receive, agree to • exclude	• I accept your explanation. • Everyone except you may go.
• adapt • adopt	• change to suit the circumstances • make one's own	• Adapt your reading style to the nature of the reading that is assigned. • You had better adopt a new method.
• adverse averse	• unfavourable • opposed to, reluctant to do	• The adverse road conditions made travel impossible. • Many of us are averse to homework.
• advice • advise	• helpful suggestions • offer advice	• Will you give us your advice? • No, I cannot advise you.
• affect • effect	• influence • result	• A blow to the head can affect memory. • One effect of a blow to the head is memory loss.
• effective • affective	• influential • related to the emotions	• He was an effective president. • Depression is a serious affective illness.
• aggravate • irritate, annoy	• make worse • bother, harass, make impatient or angry	• Loss of sleep aggravated his illness. • Your silly laugh is irritating. Are you trying to annoy us?
• all ready • already	• completely prepared • an adverb meaning *before now*	• She is all ready for the trip. • Three of us have already left.
• all together • altogether	• everyone is present • an adverb meaning *completely*	• We are all together in this picture. • Well! I was altogether confused.
• allude • elude	• refer to something (see allusion) • avoid, slip away from	• He alluded to Shakespeare's verse. • The fox eluded the hounds.
• allusion • reference • quotation	• indirect mention • clear, direct mention • repetition of exact spoken or written words	• He made an allusion to his mysterious journey. • He referred to page one, paragraph 3. • He quoted the first lines of his orders.
• allusion • illusion	• indirect mention • idea or image that is not what it appears	• He made an allusion to his mysterious journey. • The ghost was an illusion produced by the moonlight.
• among • between	• usually used of several • usually used of two	• The inheritance was divided among the five sisters. • The inheritance was divided between Manfred and Louisa.
• ante • anti	• before • against	• Antebellum refers to the period before the American Civil War. • He made an anti-war speech.

Copyright Protected

• anxious	• worried	• He is anxious about his marks.
• eager	• enthusiastic and impatient	• He is eager to hear his results.
• anyone	• an indefinite pronoun	• Anyone may answer the question.
• any one	• a noun phrase similar in meaning to the pronoun *anyone*; it emphasizes the number; *any* is an adjective, *one* is a pronoun	• Any one of your poems may be submitted.
• avoid	• stay away from	• He wishes to avoid trouble.
• avert	• prevent	• We may be able to avert war by preparing for it.
• awhile	• a brief time; do not use with *for*	• We sat awhile and rested.
• a while	• a period of time; used with *for*	• I shall be gone for a while.
• bad	• an adjective	• I feel bad about that.
• badly	• an adverb	• He behaved badly.
• beside	• by the side of	• The spoon is beside the cup.
• besides	• in addition to	• Besides, it makes a good joke.
• bring	• bring here	• Bring your friend when you come to visit.
• take	• take there	• Take your coat with you when you go.
• can	• is able to	• You can go wherever you want.
• may	• has permission to	• You may not ignore the traffic laws.
• capital	• main, most important	• Victoria is a capital city.
• capitol	• a building for lawmakers to meet	• The Capitol houses the US Congress.
• climatic	• refers to climate	• Vancouver has a mild climate; climatic variation is temperate.
• climactic	• highest moment	• At the climactic moment in the play, the fire alarm went off.
• complement	• something that completes something else	• Our ship now has a full complement of sailors.
• compliment	• praise	• We complimented the conductor.
• conscience	• awareness of right and wrong	• The thief's conscience began to trouble him.
• conscious	• awake and aware	• When you are awake, you are conscious.
• censor	• prohibit from publication	• Despite lip service to free speech, unpopular views are frequently censored.
• censure	• condemn	• The principal censured their unprincipled actions.
• continual	• happening over and over	• In this town, rain falls continually.
• continuous	• uninterrupted, without stopping	• The rain fell continuously for five days.
• council	• group of administrators or advisors	• The council will meet to decide.
• councilor	• a council member	• All the councilors must be present.
• counsel	• advise	• I counselled him to stay in school.
• counselor	• an advisor	• I also advised him to see the school counselor.
• disinterested	• not favouring one side or another, without bias	• We expect judges to be disinterested.
• uninterested	• not interested	• She is uninterested in origami.
• duel	• a formal conflict	• The two enraged courtiers fought a duel.
• dual	• double	• This car has a dual exhaust.
• elicit	• call forth, bring out, obtain	• With great skill, the lawyer elicited a truthful response.
• illicit	• illegal	• We fear he has been dealing in illicit drugs.
• eminent	• distinguished, famous	• An eminent professor lectured on wave dynamics.
• imminent	• about to happen	• Disaster is imminent. Take immediate precautions.
• ensure	• make sure something will happen	• Please ensure that enough supplies are stockpiled.
• insure	• take precautions in case something happens	• We will insure against disaster by being prepared.

• every one • everyone	• noun phrase • pronoun	• Every one of the books is waterlogged. • Everyone please listen.
• every day • everyday	• noun phrase • adjective	• We work hard every day. • He wore his everyday clothes to the party.
• explicit • implicit	• clear, detailed • not stated, but understood	• Even though they were given explicit instructions, they still got it wrong. • Their distaste for the job was implicit in their actions.
• farther • further	• often used for used for distance • additional	• Go one mile farther. • Take further steps.
• few • little	• use with things that can be numbered • use with things that cannot be numbered	• We saw few cars on our way. • Even so, he took little care with his work.
• fewer • less	• as above • as above	• Our goal is to have fewer cars on the road. • Our goal is less pollution.
• good • well	• an adjective • an adverb	• He always did good work. • He always worked well.
• imply • impute • infer	• suggest • to attribute something (often negatively) to someone • come to a conclusion	• Are you implying that I am lying? • He imputes dishonesty to every politician. • I infer that this experiment has been successful.
• ingenious • ingenuous	• clever and skilful • foolishly simple and trusting	• That is an ingenious invention. • She is ingenuous enough to still trust him.
• lay • lie • learn • teach	• transitive verb: I, you, we, they lay (laid, have laid) a parcel on a table; he, she, it lays (laid, has laid) a parcel on the shelf • intransitive verb: I, you, we, they lie (lay, have lain) down to sleep; he, she, it lies (lay, has lain) down to sleep • acquire knowledge • give knowledge	• Just lay that parcel over there on the counter. • When I go to bed, I lie down. • I can learn that quickly. • We learn best when we teach.
• literally • figuratively	• exact, precise, the true meaning; without exaggeration • not exact and factual; used to suggest similarities	• I have literally no money; my pockets are empty. • When I said that I wouldn't take a million dollars for that horse, I spoke figuratively. Of course we can agree on a price.
• loose • lose	• not tight • fail to keep, not have, be defeated	• I have a loose tooth. • Even though we lost the fight, let's not lose our sense of humour.
• medium • media	• medium is the singular • media is the plural	• Television is one medium of communication. • Television, newspapers, and radio are examples of communications media.
• nauseated • nauseous	• feeling sick • sickening	• That smell makes me feel nauseated. I'm afraid I might be sick. • That smell is nauseous.
• number • amount	• use with things that can be counted • use with things that cannot be counted	• I'll take a number of those books. • We have a large amount of grain stockpiled for emergencies.

Copyright Protected

• phenomenon • phenomena • phenomenal	• a remarkable thing or event • plural of phenomenon • amazing	• That young singer is an absolute phenomenon. • Yes, we've had quite a few phenomena like her lately. • That was a phenomenal series of home runs.
• precede • proceed	• come before • go ahead	• Youth precedes old age. • Let us proceed to the next point.
• prescribe • proscribe	• order • forbid	• I prescribe exercise and fresh air. • Performance enhancing drugs are absolutely proscribed.
• principal • principle	• most important • basic belief or standard	• The principal part is this one. • I can not yield on this point. It is a matter of principle.
• quote • quotation	• verb • noun	• Let me quote her exact words. • A quotation consisting of six lines of Shakespeare opened the play.
• raise • rise	• transitive verb • intransitive verb	• Raise your hand. • The sun rises in the morning.
• real • really	• adjective • adverb	• That is a real jewel. • You really have worked hard.
• rebut • refute	• dispute, disagree, make an answer • disprove	• To rebut is to make an argument against something, but not necessarily successfully. • If something is refuted, then it is shown to be false.
• set • sit	• place • rest upon	• Set the chair in the corner. • Sit on this chair over here.
• since • because	• a preposition used in an adverbial phrase showing time; or a subordinate conjunction • a subordinate conjunction	• Since yesterday, she has been working. • Since you are late, you must sign in. • Because you are late, you must sign in.
• that • which	• *that* introduces a restrictive clause, an essential part of the idea in the sentence • *which* introduces a non-restrictive clause, a non-essential part that could be removed from the sentence	• Here are the reports that you ordered. • My new book, which I promised to give to you, is missing.
• their • they're • there • there're	• possessive pronoun • contraction of *they are* • adverb, pronoun, interjection • non-standard contraction imitating speech	• Their car is smashed. • They're feeling bad about it. • We'll go there. There are three muffins left. There! Now you've done it! • There're four days left.
• to • too • two	• preposition • adverb • number	• Let's go to town. • You are too harsh. I want that one, too. • Two dogs barked.
• tortuous • torturous	• winding, twisted • like torture	• The lawyer's tortuous arguments confused everyone. • Twelve hours of torturous effort followed.
• unique • unusual	• one of a kind (never add a modifier to unique) • not common	• The Cullinan diamond is unique. • Any very large diamond is unusual.
• whose • who's	• interrogative pronoun • contraction of *who is*	• Whose diamond is this? • Who's this strange man?
• your • you're	• possessive pronoun • contraction of you are	• Your Rolls Royce has arrived. • No doubt you're glad to see it.

Not for Reproduction

EXAMPLES OF CONJUNCTIVE ADVERBS

Adverbs like these can be used with a semicolon to join independent clauses into compound sentences.

For example:
- We have presented our case completely; on the other hand, there is no telling how the judge will respond.
- I like your pitch; however, it sounds too much like an *Indiana Jones* movie.

Here are some common conjunctive adverbs.

accordingly	incidentally	on the contrary
as a result	indeed	on the other hand
at the same time	instead	otherwise
consequently	likewise	similarly
finally	meanwhile	so far
for example	moreover	still
for instance	namely	thereafter
furthermore	nevertheless	therefore
hence	next	thus
however	nonetheless	undoubtedly
in fact	of course	

EXAMPLES OF SUBORDINATING CONJUNCTIONS

Subordinating conjunctions introduce a subordinate clause.

For example:
- *After* the party ends, we will need to lock the hall.
- *Unless* you go, the party will be a bore.

Here are some of the more common subordinating conjunctions.

after	before	that	when
although	even though	though	where
as	if	unless	whether
as if	than	until	while
because			

USEFUL LINKING VERBS

A linking verb can be used in either of two sentence patterns:

noun + linking verb + adjective
- My new car is black.
- She turned green.
- Our well ran dry.

noun + linking verb + noun
- My aunt is the ombudsman.
- Nevertheless, they remain fools.
- Our efforts proved futile.

Linking Verbs Expressing a *State of Being*	Linking Verbs Expressing a *Change in State*
appear be feel lay look remain seem smelled sound stay taste	become get grow fall prove run turn

COMMONLY USED IRREGULAR VERBS[1]

Most lists of irregular verbs are arranged in alphabetical order. Although that order has its uses, it does make the irregular verbs appear to be a random collection of variations. Because the following lists of irregular verbs have been sorted to show the patterns of variation, they can be more easily used for review and study. For example, the first list illustrates how many verbs do not change.

Many people who speak English as their mother tongue do not know all the common English irregular verbs. Use these lists to check your knowledge.

1	Base Verb	Simple Past	Past Participle	1	Base Verb	Simple Past	Past Participle
	burst	burst	burst		let	let	let
	cast	cast	cast		put	put	put
	cost	cost	cost		quit	quit	quit
	cut	cut	cut		read	read	read
	fit	fit	fit		set	set	set
	hit	hit	hit		shut	shut	shut
	hurt	hurt	hurt		spread	spread	spread

[1] There are variations, some literary, some in common use. There are also Americanisms, such as dove used as the past tense of dive. However, students may confidently use the verb forms in these lists.

2	Base Verb	Simple Past	Past Participle	2	Base Verb	Simple Past	Past Participle
	bend	bent	bent		make	made	made
	bind	bound	bound		mean	meant	meant
	bring	brought	brought		meet	met	met
	build	built	built		pay	paid	paid
	buy	bought	bought		say	said	said
	catch	caught	caught		seek	sought	sought
	deal	dealt	dealt		sell	sold	sold
	dive	dived	dived		send	sent	sent
	feed	fed	fed		shine	shone	shone
	feel	felt	felt		shoot	shot	shot
	fight	fought	fought		sit	sat	sat
	find	found	found		sleep	slept	slept
	hang	hung	hung		spend	spent	spent
	hang[2]	hanged	hanged		stand	stood	stood
	hold	held	held		stick	stuck	stuck
	have	had	had		strike	struck	struck
	hear	heard	heard		sweep	swept	swept

[2] Hang, hanged, hanged—this verb is used only when referring to execution by hanging.

keep	kept	kept		swing	swung	swung
lay	laid	laid		teach	taught	taught
lead	led	led		tell	told	told
leave	left	left		think	thought	thought
lend	lent	lent		understand	understood	understood
light	lit	lit		win	won	won
lose	lost	lost				

3	Base Verb	Simple Past	Past Participle
	begin	began	begun
	drink	drank	drunk
	ring	rang	rung
	sing	sang	sung
	sink	sank	sunk
	spring	sprang	sprung
	swim	swam	swum

4	Base Verb	Simple Past	Past Participle
	arise	arose	arisen
	drive	drove	driven
	ride	rode	ridden
	rise	rose	risen
	write	wrote	written

5	Base Verb	Simple Past	Past Participle
	break	broke	broken
	choose	chose	chosen
	speak	spoke	spoken
	steal	stole	stolen
	wake	woke	woken

6	Base Verb	Simple Past	Past Participle
	fall	fell	fallen
	see	saw	seen
	shake	shook	shaken
	take	took	taken
	undertake	undertook	undertaken

7	Base Verb	Simple Past	Past Participle
	become	became	become
	come	came	come
	overcome	overcame	overcome
	run	ran	run

8	Base Verb	Simple Past	Past Participle
	eat	ate	eaten
	forbid	forbade	forbidden
	forget	forgot	forgotten
	forgive	forgave	forgiven
	freeze	froze	frozen
	get	got	gotten (got)
	give	gave	given
	hide	hid	hidden

Copyright Protected

9	Base Verb	Simple Past	Past Participle
	bear	bore	borne
	beat	beat	beaten
	blow	blew	blown
	do	did	done
	draw	drew	drawn
	fly	flew	flown
	grow	grew	grown
	know	knew	known
	tear	tore	torn
	throw	threw	thrown
	wear	wore	worn
	withdraw	withdrew	withdrawn

10	Base Verb	Simple Past	Past Participle
	be	was (were)	been
	go	went	gone
	lie	lay	lain
	show	showed	shown
	slay	slew	slain

KINDS OF PRONOUNS

You should be able to recognize the different kinds of pronouns.

Kinds of Pronouns	Examples	Example Sentences
Demonstrative	this, that, these, those	I want to enter *this* in the exhibition.
Interrogative	who, whom, which, what, whoever, whomever, whichever, whatever	*Who* said that?
Relative	who, whom, that, which, whoever, whomever, whichever	Choose *whichever* you like.
Indefinite	all, another, any, anybody, anyone, anything, each, everybody, everyone, everything, few, many, nobody, none, one, several, some, somebody, someone	*Many* have asked that question.
Reflexive	myself, yourself, herself, himself, itself, ourselves, yourselves, themselves	She did the job *herself*. He wanted the land for *himself*.
Intensive	myself, yourself, herself, himself, itself, ourselves, yourselves, themselves	The professor *himself* was not sure of the answer.

Notice the **reflexive** pronouns. These are often used incorrectly. The examples in the chart show the correct uses of the reflexive pronoun. When the reflexive is used immediately after the noun then it is an **intensifier**.

CREDITS

Every effort has been made to provide proper acknowledgment of the original source and to comply with copyright law. However, some attempts to establish original copyright ownership may have been unsuccessful. If copyright ownership can be identified, please notify Castle Rock Research Corp so that appropriate corrective action can be taken.

Reading and Writing

"Stars," Marjorie Pickthall

"When I Heard the Learn'd Astronomer," Walt Whitman

Practice Test 1

Excerpt from "The New Globe Theatre," Anonymous

"On the Future of Poetry," Henry Austin Dobson

Excerpt from "Stories of Gods and Heroes: The Wedding Feast," Anonymous

Excerpt from "The Game of Billiards," Alphonse Daudet

Excerpt from "A Critical Response to Alphonse Daudet's 'A Game of Billiards,'" George Pellissier, from "The Literary Movement in France in the Nineteenth Century," (1893)

"When to Her Lute Corrina Sings," Thomas Campion

Excerpt from "Oedipus the King," Sophocles

Excerpt from "Romeo and Juliette," William Shakespeare

"Part II: Nature XII," Emily Dickinson

Excerpt from "Eleonora," Edgar Allan Poe

Practice Test 2

Excerpt from "Emma," Jane Austen

Excerpt from "Love and Fashion," Frances Burney

Excerpt from "The Mysterious Marriage," Harriet Lee

Excerpt from "Eve's Ransom," George Gissing

Excerpt from "On Board the Typhoon," Anonymous

Excerpt from "Letters from England," Anonymous

"Sonnet CXXX," William Shakespeare

Excerpt from "Wastelands," Samuel Butler

"You Had Two Girls," Duncan Campbell Scott

"Stars," Marjorie Pickthall

Some images in this book are from clipart.com copyright © 2013 Clipart.com, a division of Getty Images.

Copyright Protected

NOTES

NOTES

![Alberta flag] **ALBERTA • CANADA**

BOOK ORDERING
INFORMATION
SENIOR HIGH SCHOOL TITLES

Castle Rock Research offers the following resources to support Alberta students. You can order any of these materials online at:

www.castlerockresearch.com/store

SOLARO.com - Study Online		The KEY		SNAP	Prob Solved	Class Notes
$29.95 ea.*		**$29.95 ea.***		**$29.95 ea.***	**$19.95 ea.***	**$19.95 ea.***
Biology 30	Mathematics 30-1	Biology 30	Mathematics 30-1	Biology 20	Biology 20	Biology 20
Biology 20	Mathematics 30-2	Biology 20	Mathematics 30-2	Chemistry 30	Chemistry 30	Chemistry 30
Chemistry 30	Mathematics 30-3	Chemistry 30	Mathematics 20-1	Chemistry 20	Chemistry 20	Chemistry 20
Chemistry 20	Mathematics 20-1	Chemistry 20	Mathematics 10 C	Mathematics 30-1	Mathematics 30-1	Mathematics 30-1
Physics 30	Mathematics 20-2	English 30-1	Social Studies 30-1	Mathematics 30-2	Mathematics 30-2	Mathematics 30-2
Physics 20	Mathematics 20-3	English 30-2	Social Studies 30-2	Mathematics 31	Mathematics 31	Mathematics 31
Science 30	Mathematics 20-4	English 20-1	Social Studies 20-1	Mathematics 20-1	Mathematics 20-1	Mathematics 20-1
Science 20	Mathematics 10 C	English 10-1	Social Studies 10-1	Mathematics 10 C	Mathematics 10 C	Mathematics 10 C
Science 10	Mathematics 10-3	Physics 30		Physics 30	Physics 30	Physics 30
English 30-1	Mathematics 10-4	Physics 20		Physics 20	Physics 20	Physics 20
English 30-2	Social Studies 30-1	Science 10		Science 10	Science 10	Science 10
English 20-1	Social Studies 30-2					
English 20-2	Social Studies 20-1					
English 10-1	Social Studies 10-1					
English 10-2						

Prices do not include taxes or shipping.

Study online using **SOLARO,** with access to multiple courses available by either a monthly or an annual subscription.

The KEY Study Guide is specifically designed to assist students in preparing for unit tests, final exams, and provincial examinations.

The **Student Notes and Problems (SNAP) Workbook** contains complete explanations of curriculum concepts, examples, and exercise questions.

The **Problem Solved** contains exercise questions and complete solutions.

The **Class Notes** contains complete explanations of curriculum concepts.

If you would like to order Castle Rock resources for your school, please visit our school ordering page:

www.castlerockresearch.com/school-orders/